Operation Melt

How I Used Life-
Changing Project
Management to Lose Over
100 Pounds In Under a Year

Tony Weaver

First edition March 2019

ISBN 978-0-578-48102-9 (ebook)
ISBN 978-1-092-64460-0 (amazon.com paperback)

Published by Operation Melt LLC
Columbus, OH
tony@OperationMelt.com

www.OperationMelt.com

I am not a doctor or a dietician. The information I provide is based on my personal experience. Any recommendations I may make about weight training, nutrition, supplements or lifestyle, or information provided to you in this book, in person or on my website should be discussed between you and your doctor because working out involves risks.

This information does not take the place of professional medical advice.

I Did It

I didn't come from greatness.

I didn't think I deserved it.

I didn't make it a priority because I thought I would fail so I didn't try.

I let it get the upper hand and it was trying to kill me.

Then it all changed!

I was done, embarrassed and ready.

I made a decision.

I knew why I wanted it.

I made it a priority (obsession?).

I worked my ass off.

I won!

I F—KING DID IT!!!

Because I am completely amazing!

Now... I can do anything!

Acknowledgements

I did it but I didn't do it alone!

My *Operation Melt* weight loss and fitness journey and the creation of this book was a team effort. I relied on a number of direct and indirect supporters without whom I would never have been successful. While I can't possibly thank everybody here I wanted to recognize and voice my appreciation for a few of my biggest supporters.

I want to start by thanking my wife Liz. Throughout my weight loss journey, while writing this book and through every other moment of my life she is the support system that keeps me going. Without her infinite patience while listening to me drone on and on about my daily metrics, her willingness to edit my book for me, her creative insights and her unconditional love I wouldn't have completed this journey, launched my blog, wrote this book (both her idea) or be anywhere near as happy in life. Liz, I love you and thank you!

Next I want to thank my team of experts. To my doctor, Charlie, I sincerely appreciate the push that got this journey started and all the support along the way. You helped me accomplish something I have always wanted and never thought possible and I did it in a safe and healthy way. Similarly I want to thank my trainer, Teresa, and the Fitness Loft family for helping me take my fitness journey to the next level — 100 pounds loss was just the start of my success.

Then there is my cheering section - my friends and family. You were there to listen, to recognize my progress, to give me advice and to watch the whole journey unfold. Your commitment to my success is appreciated more than you can know.

I also want to say a big thank you to a <u>big</u> group of people who have no idea that you helped me accomplish this goal. To every person who asked "are you losing weight," who said "you are looking good," who said "you are just melting away" or asked me "what's your secret?" And, especially, those who said "you have inspired me and I have started my own journey." You gave me an additional push every day — that is momentum and I needed it!

A big shout out to the coffee shops and restaurants that let me use your space and your WiFi while I was writing this book. Without your facilities, Winan's Coffee & Chocolates in particular, I may not have had the focus (or caffeine) necessary to finish!

Finally I want to recognize something bigger than me. There are powers in this universe that gave me the kick in the ass to start this journey. Those same powers also decided I needed some alone time to really kick it into high gear, to write this book and to rekindle my relationship with myself. These powers helped me turn a lay-off into a life changing sabbatical. Sometimes the universe just knows!

Table of Contents

Part 1: Introduction..8

About Me...9

About This Book..18

Project Management 101 23

Part 2: Operation Melt Project Management Plan..
32

Initiation Phase: Are You Really Doing This?...................33

Project Charter: Make A Decision & Make A Commitment..
35

Business Case: Why Is Fitness Important To You Right
Now?..47

America Has A Fitness Problem 52

Planning Phase: How Are You Going to Make This
Happen? 57

Do Your Research: The Basics Of Weight Loss 61

As-is Process Mapping: Your Fitness Audit....................68

Project Scope: What Will You And Won't You Do?...........75

Project Plan: How And When Are You Going To Do It?...85

Communication Plan: Who Are You Going To Tell And
Involve?..93

Execution Phase: Let's Make This Happen!....................98

Calories In: Fitness Starts In The Kitchen....................101

Calories Out: You Have To Get Moving 116

Monitoring & Controlling Phase: Staying The Course.....131

Motivation: Stay Committed, Stay Focused, You Will Win!.
134

Progress Tracking: Monitoring Your KPIs 143

Progress Reporting: Talk About Your Success, Even With Yourself...155

Managing Issues & Risks: Staying On Course 159

Managing Changes: Sometimes Things Happen.............166

Closure Phase: You Did It! 174

Transition To Maintenance Mode: Keeping The Weight Off 178

Project Hindsight: What Did You Learn?.......................184

Part 3: Operation Melt Hindsight Report..........188

What Is A Hindsight Report 189

Project Recap: My Results..191

Lessons Learned 202

Lesson 1: This Is A Journey, It Is Going To Take Time ..205

Lesson 2: This Journey Is Both Physical And Mental 208

Lesson 3: There Are Going To Be Lots Of Setbacks 216

Lesson 4: Equipment Matters 224

Lesson 5: You Aren't In This Alone - That's Good & Bad 229

Lesson 6: There Are Going To Be Surprises....................237

Lesson 7: Clothes Are An Issue 249

Lesson 8: Yes, You Can Indulge... Mindfully 254

Lesson 9: Nothing Motivates More Than Results...........264

Lesson 10: I Am Amazing And You Are Too!..................269

Part 4: Operation Melt Phase 2.........................274

Well... Now What? 275

Post-Audit: 9 Months Later 279

Part 1: Introduction

About Me

My name is Tony and I am just a guy living a normal, middle class, urban life in Columbus, Ohio. I have been married to my wife Liz for nearly eighteen years after being best friends for five years before becoming more. I work a demanding job leading a project management office for a retail organization. We do normal things outside of work and really enjoy our lives.

If this was the main point of this book, it would be pretty boring, huh? Well, it isn't. There is more to my story... something more unusual. The unusual thing about me stems from a decision I made.

On June 15, 2017, I decided to get healthy, and I then lost over 100 pounds in just nine months!

After living my entire 40-year life very overweight (obese, to be honest), I decided that I was going to lose more than 100 pounds in less than a year. One-hundred pounds was nearly a third of my total body weight when I started this journey.

Not only did I decide that I wanted to quickly lose weight and keep it off, but my goal was much bigger than that. I did not want to consider drugs or surgery even once, that was completely off the radar for me. I also was not going to consider a fad diet to accomplish my goal. In fact, I was not going to use somebody else's plan at all; this had to happen my way. Plus, there was one other thing that was very important to me...

I was not willing to give up things that I enjoy in order to achieve my goal!

My wife and I both had jobs that required us to work late and daily meal prep wasn't something we did regularly, so we dined out about five (or more) days per week and didn't want that to change. I enjoy foods that are not considered "health food" by any stretch of the imagination. I love to cook and eat barbecue and I am a carnivore through and through. One of my favorite foods is pizza, and that was not going to disappear from my life. Plus, I enjoy beer, wine and bourbon, and I was not planning to give up any of that.

So, there I was, embarking on a journey with a big goal and lots of constraints. These things together could have been the recipe for failure. This could have been a flash in the pan for a couple of weeks of effort, ultimately ending with me reverting back to old behaviors without achieving my goal. This is an all-too-common story and result for millions of people each year.

I knew that I needed to be different, I needed to succeed, and I needed to figure out a plan that worked for me. So I turned to something that has always worked for me every time I need to accomplish a big goal. I turned to project management!

I have been a project manager for well over a decade and have managed all kinds of projects. I have managed technology projects, construction projects, process improvement projects, non-profit initiatives and many others. I am a certified project manager who is very familiar with multiple methodologies and best practices. So, I used my project management toolbox to manage my weight loss project.

It worked! Project management was the secret to my weight loss!

I did NOT fail! I did not meet my goal of 100 pounds in a year... I did it in just nine months! And, as of writing this book, I have not only kept it off, but I have kept going.

Since a picture is worth a thousand words, I want to share a picture with you to help tell my story. This is a side-by-side comparison of my professional headshot before I started my journey and then after the eight-month point in the journey when I had reached the 96 pounds lost mark.

This is one of my proudest accomplishments in my life and it wasn't easy. But, at the same time, it wasn't as hard as you may expect. I built a great plan for myself and I think you can be successful with your own journey if you follow some of these basic principles.

Now, I want to help you to succeed with your fitness journey!

Millions of Americans struggle with their weight and I believe it is one of the top causes of unhappiness in people's lives. People are unhappy with their weight, their body, their health or their fitness. So, these millions of Americans embark on weight loss journeys each year (usually in January) and ultimately fail. Then people are unhappy with their failure and double down on their old habits as a coping mechanism. It is a deadly cycle and leads people to feel hopeless.

The reasons that people fail in their fitness journeys are many. The reasons vary widely from person to person, but some of the common mistakes are:

1.   Not having a realistic goal

2.   Not pausing to figure out why fitness is really important

3.   Not prioritizing fitness over other commitments and distractions

4.   Not knowing how to be successful

5.   Looking for a quick fix or fad diet as an easy solution

6.   Joining expensive programs where the cost outweighs the value

7.   Choosing a plan that is unsustainable or incompatible with life

8.   Not seeing immediate progress

All of these are easy mistakes to make and can lead to failure. But, I managed to design a program for myself that mitigated all of these risks and these fitness-killers didn't bring me down.

My goal for this book is to share my process with you and help you be successful too. It took me more than forty years to start my journey and less than a year to get into the best shape of my life. Plus, I enjoyed the process and couldn't be happier. Well, I may have been happier had I started ten or twenty years before or avoided the problem completely.

What the heck is Operation Melt?

I want to pause to explain why I call this book *Operation Melt*. As I started making visible progress in my journey, many people started noticing. I often got comments like, "You are just melting away!" And people were right, I was effectively melting away before my very eyes.

I have learned through many years of project management that long-term projects work better when they are branded. Branding a project makes people feel like they are part of something, and it makes it easier to talk about the project to others. So I took my own advice and best practice, and I started calling my journey *Operation Melt*.

Once it became clear that I was accomplishing something big, I decided to start telling my story in real time. So, I started a website and blog (OperationMelt.com) to report on my progress along the way and built a few diehard followers. As I will talk about later, people can be really supportive and want to know how you are doing and, more importantly, how you are making it happen. I also created a Twitter account for *Operation Melt* and started #OperationMelt as a way of tagging items related to my fitness journey.

Caution: I am not a doctor!

In this book I am sharing the process, the concepts, the lessons and best practices that worked for me during my fitness journey. I firmly believe that many of these items can be applied to your journey and will help you be successful too. But, not everything in this book will work for all people. The results I have experienced may differ materially from the results that you experience - both good and bad. So, proceed with caution and make sure to do what works for you, not just what worked for me.

Also, I just described who I am, my background, my personal and professional life earlier in this section. You may notice that I didn't say I was a doctor, because I am not. You may also have noticed that I didn't say that I am a personal trainer or fitness consultant either, because I am not. I am just a guy who built a fitness plan for himself that worked and wants to share this plan with you. But, as you will learn later in my story, I consulted my doctor and took him as a partner in my journey. You should do this too and make sure that you are approaching your journey in a safe and healthy manner.

Next, let me tell you a little bit about what to expect in this book.

I really want to get healthier but it is way too easy to keep doing what I am doing instead of fixing it. I want to get better and have to challenge myself to do so. I want to change, I want to win and I want to be better!

OPERATION MELT
WEEK 1

About This Book

As I mentioned before, the secret to my success in my fitness journey was using project management techniques to manage my weight loss. I am presenting my journey and plan to you in the book using the project management framework set forth by the Project Management Institute (PMI). I will talk more about project management in the next section. But, before we get there, I want to talk about the four parts of this book.

Part 1: Introduction

Part 1 of this book is all about introducing me and my journey as well as helping you navigate this book. Also, since this book uses a project management process as a framework, I will spend a couple of pages explaining Project Management 101 to provide some context.

Part 2: Operation Melt Project Management Plan

Part 2 will discuss the actual process I used to achieve my goals - the process that I think would work well for your journey too! I will talk about how I planned, executed, tracked and continually improved along the way. This section is structured around project management phases and activities that I will talk more about in the next chapter.

Part 3: Operation Melt Project Hindsight Report

At the end of every project, the project manager will conduct a lessons-learned meeting and then create a hindsight report of some kind. The hindsight report will present the results of the project including what was accomplished and not accomplished, schedule, budget and other results. Plus, the hindsight report will include the most important lessons learned in the project that can be leveraged for future projects.

In Part 3, I have included my project hindsight report for my *Operation Melt* project. I will review my actual results from the project. Plus, I will share the lessons I learned throughout my journey. I encountered lots of surprises, both good and bad, and I want to help prepare you for those surprises in your journey.

Part 4: Operation Melt Phase 2

In the final part of the book, I am going to talk about two words that are very familiar to project managers: "Phase 2." The nature of projects is that they have a defined starting and ending point and they don't go on forever. By definition this means that there is a finite number of things that can be accomplished in a project.

There are multiple approaches for accomplishing more than what was initially planned to accomplish in a project. One approach is to continue to add new items to the project (known as "scope creep") and allow the project to become longer and more expensive in order to address those items. Sometimes, this leads to a phenomenon known as "the project that never ends." It is very costly in time, money and in morale because the project team can never really claim victory. As such, this is usually not the right approach.

Alternatively, the items that don't get addressed within the project are addressed in a future phase. That means that you let the project come to an end as planned and the team can celebrate the victory based on the initial goal. Then, if the additional items are really worth pursuing, a "follow-on project" can be tacked on immediately after the initial project is done. This follow-on project is often referred to as "Phase 2."

Your fitness journey works the same way. You started out with a goal that you wanted to achieve, and you are going to achieve that goal. But, along the way, you are going to identify more things that you want to accomplish; this is good! So, you should get to the finish line on your original goal and celebrate your success. Then, start working on the other things that you have decided to pursue.

In the final part of the book, I am going to talk about my Phase 2 goals and what comes next for me. Some of these new goals for me are things that I would have viewed as completely unattainable just a few short months before!

I want to share one final note before we get started. Between each chapter I have included a quote. These quotes are things that I wrote in my personal journal and / or published to my blog throughout the course of my *Operation Melt* project. Each quote is a summary of the events that occurred during one week of my journey. Some of the quotes are glimpses into how I was thinking or feeling along the way. Some are happy and celebratory quotes and some are not. My hope is that these quotes help you get more of an "insider's view" of the realities of my journey.

I am focusing on losing weight, eating better, exercising more and de-stressing, because I am tired of being so overweight. It has annoyed me for years, and the time is now!

OPERATION MELT
WEEK 2

Project Management 101

The Project Management Institute (PMI) produces a publication entitled *A Guide to the Project Management Body of Knowledge* or more commonly referred to as the *PMBOK Guide*. This publication effectively is the standard for project management leveraged by project managers around the world. This guide defines standard terminology, processes and best practices for project management.

Throughout this book, when I refer to project management processes and concepts, I am referring to the items set forth in the *PMBOK Guide*. This includes defining what a "project" really is. You see the word "project" everywhere and it is used to describe many different things. But not everything in life is a project, particularly for the purposes of this book. When I use the word "project," I am referring to the following definition:

A project is a temporary endeavor undertaken to create a unique product, service or result.

Being a "temporary endeavor" means that a project, including your weight loss project, has both a starting and an ending point. The starting point is where you are when you decide to begin your fitness journey. The ending point is when you have achieved the goal you set out to achieve, usually a target weight or amount of weight lost. As I mentioned before, achieving your goal doesn't mean that you have to be *done* per se, but that you are done with the original project and can move onto Phase 2.

Creating "a unique product, service or result" means that a project is something you do in order to accomplish a specific goal. A project is not something you do every day in the course of your life. So, for your weight loss, the "unique product, service or result" is simply the new and improved you after reaching your goal.

For *Operation Melt*, my "project" was to lose over one-hundred pounds ("unique product, service or result") in under one year from June 15, 2017 ("temporary endeavor").

One additional important thing to note regarding the "unique product, service or result" is the use of the word "unique." Every project, by its very nature, is unique, and no two projects are ever exactly the same. There may be similarities between projects, but each project is inherently different from all other projects. Your fitness journey is no different. While there are concepts that are nearly universal in every journey, your journey and mine are different. This means that you will need to tailor the approach to fit your needs and lifestyle because your "product, service or result" is unique compared to mine.

Similar to "project", the term "project management" has taken on a number of different definitions in the world around us. I have seen the term "project manager" used to describe writers, managers, meeting facilitators, customer service reps and many other things. In those contexts, this term is probably fine, but it really doesn't work for our purposes in this book. So I will again turn to the *PMBOK Guide* for my definition for "project management."

The application of knowledge, skills, tools and techniques to project activities to meet the project requirements.

Said a little differently, project management is the work that you do in order to produce the "unique product, service or result" within the timeframe of your "temporary endeavor." This work draws from a number of different areas of a project manager's knowledge and experience in order to achieve success. The specific requirements of each project will necessitate different work to be done and will require different skills and techniques. This is where the professional expertise of the project manager is critical in order to choose the right tools from the toolbox.

While the specific tools needed for a project are unique, project managers believe that there are a set of common tools and techniques and processes that apply universally. These common tools provide a basic structure that serves as a framework for all projects. This framework is a project management process or a methodology.

At its core, the components of the project management methodology are a set of processes that are applied that usually produce a tangible item called an "artifact." Some examples of the artifacts that are produced by project management processes include a project plan, a budget, a communications plan and other common items.

The common processes within the project methodology are grouped together into a series of five process groups. These process groups represent the common stages of the lifecycle of your project. Sometimes people will refer to the process groups as project phases. Because these process groups are the basis for how the next section of this book is structured, I wanted to take a minute to describe the process groups for you. They are depicted in the following illustration.

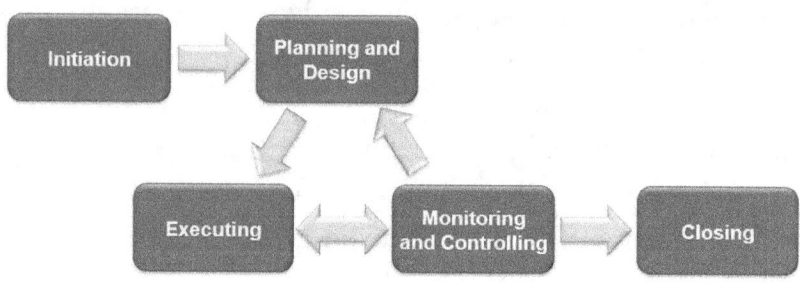

All projects start with an initiation phase. This is the phase when the project officially comes into existence. Some of the things that need to be determined during the initiation phase are the constraints for the project, the objectives and goals, and the initial timeline. For a fitness project, this is the time where you have to make a decision. Are you really going to start this journey?

The second phase of a project is the planning phase. Now that you know your objectives and constraints defined in the initiation phase, it is time to figure out how you are going to execute the project to achieve those goals. It is during this phase where you detail out the work to be done and the detailed timeline in your project plan. This is where you determine what resources you will need and what they will cost, and then you build a project budget. Plus, this is a time when you will determine how you will track progress and how you will communicate with stakeholders. For your fitness project, this is where you are going to decide how to approach your weight loss: what are you going to do, when are you going to do it, who are you going to consult and who are you going to tell?

Once you have planned your work, you need to work your plan; this is the focus of the execution phase of the project. During the execution phase, the work that was defined in your plan is performed and the real work of the work gets done. In a normal project, this is where the project manager plays more of a low-key role, but not in your fitness project. This is where you live your fitness journey and all of your hard work happens.

In parallel with the execution phase is the monitoring and controlling phase. This is where the project manager tracks progress and reacts as needed.

During this phase, the project manager continually measures Key Performance Indicators (KPIs) to evaluate how the work is progressing versus the plan. Based on the measurements, the project manager will also report progress updates to project stakeholders via a variety of status reporting mechanisms. Also, any deviations from the plan will be identified and appropriate corrective action taken. In your fitness project, this is where you will be measuring the results of the work you are doing in the execution phase and sharing your progress.

In the diagram, you may notice that planning, execution and monitoring and controlling look like they all happen at the same time. There is absolutely overlap in these activities and they are not one-time efforts. As execution is happening, progress is being measured through the monitoring and controlling efforts. New information may require adjustments to the plan or complete re-planning. This balance happens throughout the project.

Once the work of the project is complete, the project enters into the closing phase. This is where the project manager confirms that all of the work is done and wraps up the project to move on to next. Some of the key activities include transition of the project into "business as usual" or daily operations (also known as maintenance mode), closing out any contracts, releasing any project resources, archiving all of the project artifacts for future use and, most importantly, conducting the lessons learned analysis. The goal is to identify and document any lessons that were learned in the project that may be able to be applied to make future projects better. All of these lessons learned and the final report on the project status are usually documented in a hindsight report that is delivered when the project is formally closed.

Your fitness project will absolutely have a similar phase as the closing phase because you are going to meet your goal and will ultimately be done with the project portion of your effort. This is where your weight maintenance mode begins, and you must continue living your new healthy lifestyle to maintain your weight. You may even launch a new project to achieve additional fitness goals after your initial goal is met. Plus, as I am doing with this book and have been doing though OperationMelt.com, I would recommend documenting the lessons you have learned and sharing them with others. Because all fitness projects are unique, you never know how something you did or learned may help others with their own journeys. Think of it as a way to pay-it-forward and to continue to build good karma in life.

There you have it; that is project management in a nutshell and should equip you well to follow the structure of the rest of this book. As the chapters unfold, you will learn more about project management and some of the specific artifacts included in each of these phases or process groups. And now, since this is not a project management book per se, I will stop talking about how to manage projects and get into the guts of how I managed my fitness project.

I have finished my second week of my new get-healthy plan. Lots more successes this week, but a few issues have developed too.

OPERATION MELT
WEEK 3

Part 2: Operation Melt Project Management Plan

Initiation Phase: Are You Really Doing This?

Plato said, "The beginning is the most important part of the work." And he was right. In any project, the beginning is the initiation phase. This phase is all about making a decision to accomplish something and to kick off a project to do it.

In your fitness project, the initiation phase is the most important part of the work, just like Plato said. This is the case because this is the time for you to make a decision. Is this the time when you are going to get serious about your health and fitness? Are you going to commit to being successful this time? Is this really important to you?

In the initiation phase, we are going to leverage a couple of processes and produce a couple of artifacts to help you make the decision. More importantly, we are going to work on a couple of artifacts to help commit to the decision versus just saying it. This has to be important to you or you won't stick with it.

So let's make a decision, and let's make it important!

My weight throughout the week has been up and down. But, by the end of the week, I was down to 306 pounds, so I am approaching the milestone of getting under 300 pounds.

OPERATION MELT
WEEK 4

Project Charter: Make A Decision & Make A Commitment

The first artifact in the project initiation phase is the project charter. The project charter is a formal recognition that the project exists and is authorized to continue. Some of the items that are commonly included in a project charter are:

- The objectives for the project

- The reason that this project exists

- The constraints around the project. (What are the boundaries?)

- Any risks that may jeopardize the project's ability to be successful

- Any initial timeline, scope, budget or other considerations

In a business setting, the recognition that the project exists and is authorized to take action is something that gets shared with leadership and the project team. In your fitness project, the charter is really to recognize for *yourself* that your project exists and to state its goals. The charter marks a decision point in your life.

Your decision to make a change and to commit to getting fit is your moment. It is that moment in time when everything changes. It is pivotal and can literally become the decision between life and death. Your moment can be the decision between happiness or status quo. When your moment happens, make a note of it because you will want to remember it later when you have achieved your goal.

Everybody's moment is different. It can be deeply personal. Your moment will likely be brought on by an event or incident in your life. This event will cause you to pause and say, "I have to make a change!" For some people this happens when you find out you are going to become a parent. For others, it may be driven by some sort of health scare or fitness challenge (like getting winded walking up a flight of stairs). Sometimes this decision happens when you look in the mirror and really dislike, or are disappointed by, what you see.

In most cases your moment is a combination of events that all lead up to you making that pivotal decision to prioritize yourself, your health, your fitness and your happiness. In most cases your moment will not be easy for you because it requires you to tell yourself the truth. This may be truth that you have been hiding from yourself for a long time and have walled off like a fortress. The truth is that you have been failing at managing your health and/or your weight. You have made yourself the last priority. Now, you have to dig yourself out of a hole brought on by neglect. It's ok. You can fix it. But first, you have to admit it!

My moment happened over a two-week period in June of 2017. But, as I just mentioned, it was a build-up that happened over 40 years. It was a long time coming, but still was not an easy decision.

I had been overweight for my entire life — at least as far back as I can remember. I was the fat kid in school. Though my weight had its ups and downs, it was never something I was proud of for my entire life. I was embarrassed by my body image, but I kept convincing myself that my personality, my humor, my intellect, my drive and my successes made my weight unimportant.

When I was in elementary school and junior high, I continued to increase in size and was over 200 pounds in junior high. When I went to high school, I joined junior ROTC and this caused my physical activity to increase quite a bit and I was at my healthiest for my first three years of high school. But at my healthiest, I was still over 230 pounds and had a size 42 waist as a junior in high school. Then in my senior year, I was done with ROTC and that took away my physical activity.

What makes this situation worse is that it is a self-perpetuating problem. I was overweight and that led to getting picked on and bullied. Because of this, I would withdraw a bit from being social with other kids except for a few other social outcasts like me. Then I would spend my time indoors doing non-physical activities such as learning computer programming, watching television, snacking and such. As a result, I would stay big, get even bigger, and the problem would get worse. It was a viscous cycle.

My family didn't really know it was an issue because we were a pretty unhealthy family and the kids weren't the only overweight ones in the house. My dad was also dramatically overweight and was probably pushing the 400 pounds mark. At his largest, he was a size 60 waist. For every one of us, the underlying causes were very similar. Our family activity was limited to television and other equally as vigorous physical activities. Plus, based on all of the other factors in our lives, every one of us struggled with our self-esteem and confidence in our own ways, and none of us had many friends.

Compounding the lack of physical activity was our nutrition. We would often eat terrible food and often in front of the TV. We didn't always eat terribly, there was definitely healthy food in the house sometimes. We would have vegetable-heavy meals in the summer when they could be harvested from the garden and grilled out. Unfortunately, this was not always the choice we made.

Much of our nutrition issue growing up was related to a financial issue. We were a very poor family most of the time. I say most of the time because the financial situation tended to be feast or famine in our house. Most of the time, there was very little money so we were left with few healthy options. When there was money, we would celebrate the fact that there was money by splurging on pizza, buffet restaurants and the like. I am sure that my parents did the best they could with the knowledge and resources available to them, but it fell short of creating a healthy environment.

Reflecting on that time, it is actually very disappointing the level of poor health that is driven by living in poverty. Pair the health impacts of poverty with the fact that people often cannot break free from the cycle of poverty and you have a recipe for a public health disaster. Sadly, that disaster has come true in America today.

Back to the background for my moment... Through my adult life, I paid little attention to my fitness, physical activity or my nutrition. In college, I was on my own for the first time and lived it up with bad choices. Like many college kids, I started drinking alcohol which immediately adds a ton of additional calories. I was very active in student activities, but they were things like the college radio station and working in the computer lab which didn't drive me to move very much.

The alcohol was just the tip of the iceberg in poor nutritional decisions I made in college. I ate many pre-packaged foods such as boxed macaroni and cheese in my dorm room. I would consume the whole box which is about four servings. I would eat fast food with friends, and we had a go-to of ordering a triple cheeseburger at a local restaurant with large fries. We would also eat lots of pizza and chicken wings and other poor decisions.

After graduating from college, I kept building on my foundation of bad nutritional and physical activity decisions. I seldom (read, never) paid attention to the nutritional information associated with the things I was consuming. I pretty much just enjoyed the moment.

In 2001, I went to the doctor to have something checked out. I stepped on the scale and I was over 300 pounds! I had no idea! So, I spent a few weeks exercising and eating right, but quickly returned to my old behaviors. I convinced myself that I was doing fine and holding steady. My solution was to not go back to the doctor and not know for sure if I was growing or shrinking.

I was ignoring all the signs that I had a problem. I would get winded when walking up a single flight of stairs. I would sweat all the time in the summer and was absolutely miserable when it was hot out. I was snoring every night and I don't know how my wife could get any sleep. I would perpetually order meat-heavy dishes at restaurants and could always eat more - and often did. Having a very small statured wife who fills up quickly at meals often meant that I would finish what she didn't eat in addition to my own meal. Plus, I drank too much in both quantity and frequency.

I could only shop at big and tall stores and had very few clothing options. Then every couple of years, I would have to buy bigger clothes or at least ones that were the same size but fit looser. In June of 2017, I was a size 52 waist and wore a size 3XL. I was starting to find lots of 3XL clothes that weren't fitting.

Even worse, I hated how I looked when I looked in the mirror and in photos. I was way too big, and I just assumed that I would be for the rest of my life. I was happy in most other aspects of my life, so I pretty much ignored my health. Here is an example of what I saw in photos and in the mirror that I hated so much.

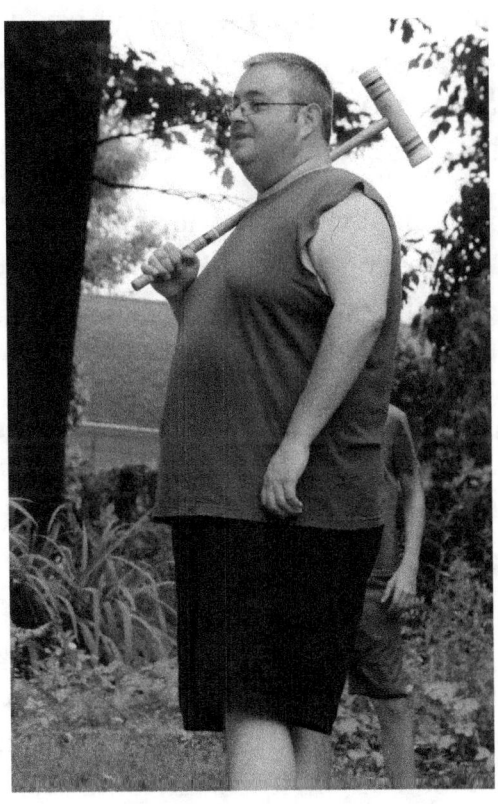

Beyond ignoring my health, I would make jokes about the severity. I would talk about the fact that my dad died at 59 and his mother at 63 and would tell Liz that she should plan for her second husband now. I would say things like, "I am overweight, eat like crap, don't exercise, drink and have a high stress job, so I am on the right path!" It was mostly a joke, but there was some seriousness built into it for sure.

The situation was terrible, irresponsible and getting worse, but I wasn't ready to turn it around. Then I turned 40 and it started to dawn on me that this was really not heading a good direction. It really started to hit me that I was in the last 20 years of my life if I go the same way as my dad and grandmother.

To this point, this is just background information and the series of events that started to set the stage for my moment. This is the 40 years of bad choices that led me to my moment in June of 2017.

My actual moment all started with one Friday night of bad decisions. I had a very draining week of job-related stress and failures. So I decided to meet Liz and some friends after work for a happy hour. We went to one of our favorite bars, and I had a few cocktails while there. Then we went to another favorite restaurant, and I had a few more cocktails. Then we went to a third restaurant and had dinner and another cocktail. I knew I had drank a bit too much, but didn't think it was anything over-the-top by any means. I went home and went to bed as per usual.

The morning after this marathon drinking and eating night was terrible! I woke up with the worst hangover of my life. The hangover was far worse than anything I had ever experienced even on those rare times where I consumed way more alcohol. It was this moment when a classic lyric from a Hank Williams, Jr. song really resonated.

"The hangovers hurt more than they used to..."

I don't know if this was a side-effect of getting older, but it was bad and a bit frightening.

Making the fear factor worse was the prolonged impacts of the bad choices. Yes, the hangover was mostly gone by that evening, but not entirely. I still had some lingering digestive issues for a few days afterwards and it took a while to get back to normal. So, I decided to do something I hadn't done since 2001, I made an appointment to see a doctor!

I walked into my first doctor's appointment in over 15 years on the morning of June 15, 2017. I sat in the waiting room and nervously completed my paperwork. This was the first of many sobering moments that day. My answers on the health questionnaires painted a very bad picture that I had never seen all in one place before. Yikes!

The nurse called me back for my exam and the first stop was at the scale. I stepped on the scale and expected to be somewhere between 300 and 305 pounds — and this would have been disappointing. I stepped on the scale and saw a number I never would have expected — 325 pounds! I was devastated when I saw that. But, little did I know, the bad news was just starting.

I went into the exam room with the nurse, and she asked me the standard set of questions. Many of my answers echoed what was on the forms that I had filled out. Again, came so much disappointment in myself.

Then the doctor came in and did his exam. We discussed a number of troubling things. He asked me about my nutrition. I said, "I don't eat great, but it isn't terrible." Together we figured out that this was incorrect. I did have some terrible habits. He asked me about how much I drink, and we determined that I needed to reduce my consumption.

My doctor then asked me about stress from work and working hours. I told him that I didn't know how many hours per week I worked because I intentionally stopped keeping track. He said, "Well, let's add it up together. Walk me through your normal week."

So, I recapped my normal work week including early morning emails and such before going into the office, my actual time in the office, lunches at my desk or in meetings, calls during my drive home and evening and weekend work at home. The doctor was diligently noting my answers as I was saying them and he quickly replied, "So you are working sixty or seventy hours per week?"

Are you kidding me, how am I working that much?!

Then he gave me the reality check. I really have to cut back on everything I am doing except for exercise. I need to increase exercise to more than zero. He told me what I already kind of knew but was avoiding, I was on a very disastrous path and needed to figure out how to make a change. Then he stole 6 vials of blood and scheduled a follow-up appointment in two weeks to get the results of bloodwork. Those results would include the moment of truth about whether or not I was showing signs of diabetes which runs in my family.

I walked out of the first appointment with my doctor very disappointed with myself. I was failing at my health! I was on a path towards the early death that I kept joking about. I had let myself get up to 325 pounds! I needed to make a change immediately and never look back. Plus, I didn't have all the information yet because there was still bloodwork to get back.

And this was my moment! This is when I made the decision to take action and do something. I just needed to figure out what that something was. I had my charter. Lose weight, lose it now and get better.

As of this morning, I crossed the 25 pounds mark and have lost a total of 26 pounds since I started. I am under 300 pounds! That's 8 percent of my body weight in just over 30 days! This is one of my biggest accomplishments ever!

OPERATION MELT
WEEK 5

Business Case: Why Is Fitness Important To You Right Now?

The next step in the initiation phase is to define your business case. I know that this may not be the order of operations for all projects and that business case may precede the charter or even precede the project. But, since this isn't a book intending to teach about project management, I am going to stick with my sequencing.

A business case is the justification for why a project needs to exist. It is normally a very financially oriented document to discuss things like expected financial benefits versus costs and the total return on investment (ROI) for the project. Sometimes the business case will talk about the larger environment in which the organization exists in order to discuss why the project is important from a competitive or regulatory perspective.

Regardless of how and when the business case is constructed, the intent is the same. It sets the stage for why this project is important to do right now. It creates a sense of urgency by discussing the risks of not doing the project and the benefits of doing the project. It is a very important document to justify the project's existence.

In your fitness project, the business case is also very important. The business case for a fitness project seeks to answer one question, "Why?" Why is it important to you to take this project on right now? Why are you focused on improving your fitness? What happens if you don't do this? Your business case, or your "why," is a tool for helping you stay committed and focused on achieving your goal.

Similar to your moment that I talked about in the last chapter when we were working on our project charter, your "why" is deeply personal. Everybody has a unique "why." No two people have exactly the same reason for starting their fitness journey. It is important for you to figure out your "why" at the beginning of your journey.

While your "why" is very personal, there are some factors that impact every one of us in America that should help make your case for fitness. In the next chapter, I will talk about how and why America has a fitness problem. The factors I describe in that chapter should be a small part of your business case and might help explain why embarking on a fitness journey is so important right now.

When I started my journey, I went through my own business case exercise based on something I read in an article. I wanted to have my "why" on paper so I could refer back to it if I started failing in my journey. The goal was to have something that was important enough to me that I would continue to make my fitness project a priority in my life over other things.

I am focusing on losing weight, eating better, exercising more and de-stressing because:

- I am tired of being so overweight. It has annoyed me for years and I just have to address it. The time is now because I hit an embarrassing level at 325 pounds.

- I am tired of only being able to shop at big-and-tall stores. I am sick of having to worry about maximum capacity on chairs I hate not being able to do things that Liz wants to do (horseback riding, zip-line, etc.) because I exceed the maximum weight.

- I am tired of glances and being thought less of because I am fat.

- I am sick of not having high self-confidence because I hate how I look to myself and others. I am sick of avoiding mirrors, pictures, doctors and the truth.

- I am over forty now and need to get into some healthier habits or face terrible consequences. My dad died at fifty-nine after a really rough ten-plus years of suffering My grandmother died at 63 after years of suffering. I don't want this to be me. I don't want to be in the last twenty years of my life yet.

- Liz is going to live to a very old age, and I don't want her to have to do it alone. I want to be there with her.

As you can see, your business case doesn't have to be long and drawn out by any means, it just has to be relevant to you. This project is going to be hard and is going to require lots of work along the way. You want to make sure you remember why you started it in the first place.

Over the past month, I have rediscovered something - numbers are very important to me. I like to be able to measure things and like to be able to trend progress using those numbers. Now I am applying this to my health, and the results are very clear.

OPERATION MELT
WEEK 6

America Has A Fitness Problem

By now we have all heard information about the terrible state of health and fitness in America. We eat terrible foods, we don't exercise, we drink, we smoke, we have high stress and we are fat.

If you want to see some staggering information, take a trip to the Centers for Disease Control (CDC) website and look at the obesity data for the US. Over a third (and approaching forty percent) of American adults are classified as obese by the CDC. It has also been projected that by 2030, at least fifty percent of American adults will be obese.

Obesity causes numerous medical conditions including many of the conditions that lead to early and preventable deaths. Conditions such as Type-Two diabetes, stroke, heart disease and some cancers are all linked to obesity. These result in huge financial and human costs that could all be avoided.

Part of the cause of the American obesity epidemic stems from how and what we eat. The US government shares some interesting statistics regarding the state of nutrition in America on the health.gov website. One of the biggest issues in our nutrition stems from what we don't eat in America: vegetables. About seventy-five percent of the US population has a diet that is too low in fruits and vegetables.

I have personally met many people, particularly men, who unapologetically talk about the fact that they don't eat vegetables. They say they don't like the taste so never eat vegetables, even lettuce and tomato on burgers. I heard somebody once say, "I am not going to eat a vegetable just to try a sauerkraut ball." Mind you, this is a breaded and deep-fried ball of sauerkraut and sausage. How do people live that way?!

In place of eating healthy fruits and vegetables, we Americans over-consume in a number of other categories. Over fifty percent of the US population is over-consuming breads and proteins instead of fruits and vegetables. Nearly all Americans also consume excessive amounts of sugars, saturated fats and sodium. All these lead to obesity and other terrible health conditions.

Not only do we eat terribly, we also don't exercise to burn those calories. Another source for some very troubling statistics is the *President's Council on Sports, Fitness and Nutrition* from the US Department of Health and Human Services. Here are some of the more relevant statistics to help you with your business case for fitness.

- Less than five percent of adults participate in thirty minutes of physical activity each day and only about three percent receive the recommended amount of physical activity each week.

- Over eighty percent of adults and adolescents do not meet their respective guidelines for both aerobic and muscle-strengthening activities.

- Children now spend more than seven and a half hours a day in front of a screen.

- Nearly thirty percent of Americans aged six or older get so little exercise that they are categorized as "physically inactive."

Nearly everybody who isn't achieving their recommended daily physical activity target will be able to give you some reason why they aren't exercising. People have a stunning ability to justify their bad behavior. But the number one excuse for not exercising is the same as the top excuse for almost anything. *I don't have time.*

Let me just say that the "I don't have time" excuse is complete B.S.! It is just a crutch that people use to get out of doing things. It is dishonest and it has to stop!

Yes, people are leading busy lives. They are rushing around to drop the kids off, to get to work for their long work day, to pick up the kids, to get to the kids' activities, and so on and so forth. But people are also rushing to get to happy hour, are sleeping late, are watching tons of television, and spending lots of time on their phones and computers. You have the time, you just have to prioritize the time.

When people are saying, "I don't have time to exercise," what they are really saying is something very different. What people are really saying, "Exercise isn't as important to me as other things because I have to work hard and don't get immediate gratification." So they choose other activities. So just stop being "too busy" and start getting moving otherwise we are all headed for a disastrous ending.

It is not easy to be fit in America because there are lots of ways that the deck is stacked against your fitness. Our on-the-go culture has caused us to choose prepackaged or fast food meals in place of cooking for ourselves with fresh, wholesome ingredients. Because the goals of these options are profit and shelf-stability instead of nutrition, these are often horrible choices. They are packed with sodium, high-fructose corn syrup, calories and fat. Sometimes it seems like companies go out of their way to try to make their foods more unhealthy and to cram in more calories and fat. These shortcuts cause early death!

Am I becoming obsessed with healthy living? Maybe a little, but I really believe this is my one chance to get better. My chance to reverse 40 years of bad decisions and keep myself alive. I am still enjoying myself and doing things I like to do. I am just trying to do better.

OPERATION MELT
WEEK 7

Planning Phase: How Are You Going to Make This Happen?

So here you are. You have decided that you are going to start a project to get yourself more fit and healthy. You have decided that it is important to you and you know why. You are ready to make this a priority and be successful. You are motivated, you are ready, and it is time to take action. So now what?

A goal without a plan is just a wish

Antoine de Saint-Exupery

You need a plan! It is time to kick off the planning phase for your fitness project. This is the phase where you will decide on your specific goals and scope for your project. You will determine your plan for what you need to do and your timeline for getting there. You will also determine how you are going to communicate with people.

In the planning phase, you are going to produce some key artifacts that will guide you through the entire remainder of your fitness journey. You will continue to leverage and continue to update and refine these artifacts until you are done and beyond. You will also use these artifacts to show yourself the progress you are making when you can't see it.

Most importantly, you are going to start by figuring out why you are overweight and opening your eyes to some facts. But, that is going to help set you up for the success that you are going to have later!

There is one caveat that needs to be called out here:

Take action now. Don't wait until your plan is finished!

Sometimes people get stuck with their goals because they are trying to design the perfect plan. They want to analyze everything exhaustively so they don't make a mistake and start down the wrong road. Before you know it, you are in analysis paralysis and have gone nowhere. Every minute you spend waiting for your plan to be done is a minute lost in actually making progress. In your fitness journey, there is an easy way to avoid this.... JUST MOVE!

Start your journey today with easy things. Go for a walk right now. Choose a healthy snack instead of the chips. Ask a friend to go for a walk with you. Take the stairs at work. Park further away tomorrow morning. There are countless ways to get started today and start racking up the quick wins. Break free from the inertia and start building momentum.

You are absolutely going to make mistakes. The plan you start on Day One will look very different on Day Thirty as you learn more. In project management this is called progressive elaboration and it is key to every single project accomplishment. Change is ok, no decision you make is undoable and nothing is uncorrectable.

So do something, and do it now! In fact, while you are reading the next chapter or two, get up and move. You can probably walk and read without crashing into a pole. Or, pause here, walk somewhere and sit down to read the next chapter. Then repeat.

Last night I had a lapse of willpower when the snacks were out during our game night. I kept eating cashews and trail mix all evening. I definitely went overboard. Next week I need to get back into a regular pattern of consumption.

OPERATION MELT
WEEK 8

60

Do Your Research: The Basics Of Weight Loss

One of the fundamental tenets of project management is that a project manager's skillset can be applied in many types of projects. Theoretically, as a project manager, whether you are building software or building a bridge, the skills required to manage the project are the same. So project management claims to be subject-matter agnostic. However, any project manager will tell you that it is easier to manage a project where you have some knowledge of the subject matter.

Occasionally as a project manager you are a subject matter expert in the domain involved in your project. When that is the case, you are well-equipped to get started building the project scope document to define what you will and won't do to achieve your goals. While this is the best-case scenario by far, it is often not the case. So, the next step, after you have started your project and understand your current process, is to do some research to get smarter about the subject matter.

The need to build some subject matter expertise in your project is absolutely a need in your fitness project. You really need to have a basic understanding of how people lose weight. Having some knowledge about how weight loss works will help you be successful with losing weight yourself. Makes sense, right?

When you are trying to learn about the basics of weight loss, there are so many resources that you could spend years reading them all. Please do not do this. When you are just getting started, you just need to have a basic understanding of the mechanics of weight loss. As you progress through your journey, I would suggest continuing to read about health and fitness on a daily basis and keep getting smarter about the subject. But to get started, you just need to know a few basics.

The first thing you will want to understand is our friend, the calorie. A calorie is a measurement of energy. When you are looking at the nutritional information on food, the number of calories in that food translates to the amount of energy that the food contains. This energy is stored in food in the protein, carbohydrates and fat contained within the food. It is helpful to start thinking of food as fuel and the number of calories as the amount of fuel within each food item.

Your body needs calories. The calories that you consume are used to fuel your basic biological functions (your brain, your heart and such,) as well as for your daily physical activity including any exercise. It may be helpful to think of your body as an engine and the calories as the fuel that makes that engine go.

The number of calories that you need every day varies from person to person based on a few different factors. First, your height and weight are a major factor in determining the number of calories that your body needs. The bigger your body, the more calories it needs just to function on a daily basis. This also means that the number of calories you need each day will decrease as you are successful with your weight loss journey.

I want to introduce a technical term now because I will be using it throughout this book as I talk about diet and exercise. That term is base metabolic rate, or BMR. Your BMR is the number of calories that your body requires (or burns) at rest every day just to power your basic biological functions.

Beyond your BMR, your daily calorie requirements are affected by your physical activity. Your body requires more calories as you are more active because you need the energy to support that extra activity. As such, if you are not very active, your daily calorie need will be lower than if you are very active. You may have heard stories of professional athletes (like Olympic swimmers) who consumed 12,000 calories in a day to help them compete. Clearly, most people should not consume anywhere near that many calories.

The number of calories that you should be consuming on a daily basis depends on your BMR (a function of your height, weight and age) plus your level of activity. For the average person who is a bit overweight and not super active your daily calorie need will be somewhere in the neighborhood of 2,000. To figure out exactly how many calories you need, there are a variety of websites that have calculators that will ask you some questions and spit out a daily calorie target. You should probably verify this target with your doctor just to be sure.

The heart of weight loss is associated with what happens when you over- or under-consume the calories that your body will burn each day. If you consume more calories than your body burns, these calories are stored by your body for future use like a battery. The battery that your body uses to store these calories is your fat cells.

Very basically said, you are overweight because you have too many calories stored as fat because you are consuming more calories than your body uses every day. So what happens if you consume fewer calories than your body needs? Well, your body has planned ahead for just such a scenario and will find these calories somewhere else. Your body will turn to the calories stored in your fat cells to offset any deficit that it needs to accommodate. This means that creating a calorie deficit will force your body to consume stored fat and your body will get smaller.

The good news about weight loss is that it is basically just a big math problem. In fact, in many ways, your weight is similar to your household budget. If you want to save money, you have to have more income than your expenses, thus creating a growing balance in your bank account. But if you are spending more than you are bringing in, your account balance will continue to drop. So to lose weight, you just need to spend more calories than you deposit and create a deficit.

Let me pause for a second and point out that there are lots of factors that I didn't discuss in this summary of losing weight. While it is very mathematical, your body is a bit more complex than that. There are a number of biological factors, such as your metabolism, that can make it easier or harder to lose weight. For example, it is easier to lose weight when you are heavier than when you are lighter. It tends to be easier for men to lose weight than it is for women to lose weight. Also, I didn't mention nutrition at all. The types of calories that you consume do, in fact, matter a great deal. These are things that may or may not impact you as you get further into your journey. But for now, I want to keep it basic so we can get your fitness project off the ground. Otherwise, we risk analysis paralysis.

Ok, back to the basics of losing weight. I mentioned that the secret to losing weight is to consume fewer calories than you burn each day. Creating this calorie deficit will cause your body to burn fat to get the calories that you need. By burning this fat, you will start losing some of the excess weight stored in these fat cells. Some people refer to this approach to weight loss as "calories in, calories out" for short.

Burning one pound of fat translates to a deficit of about 3,500 calories

Now for some good news about creating your calorie deficit - you have options. In order to create the calorie deficit that you need in order to lose weight you have two options. You can decrease the calories you take into your body by managing the foods that you consume - this is also known as dieting. You can also increase the number of calories that your body burns each day by increasing your physical activity - this is known as exercise. But the best approach and the one that I would recommend is to do both diet and exercise. (Shocking, I know!) By doing both things, it will be far easier to achieve your weight loss goals than just adjusting one side or the other.

This should be enough subject matter expertise to get you started with your weight loss journey. Now you know that losing weight is a math problem that depends on the number of calories you are taking into your body (diet) as well as the number of calories that are burning out of your body (exercise). But do you know why you are overweight or how many calories you are consuming or burning each day? Probably not... I didn't. That is where the next step in your project comes into play.

I am having problems with my morning routine for some reason this week. I am sleeping in and talking myself out of getting up and exercising. That's not good, but my plan is to get back on track tomorrow.

OPERATION MELT
WEEK 9

As-is Process Mapping: Your Fitness Audit

Do you know why you are overweight? Do you know what your ideal healthy weight is? Do you know what you weigh today? Do you know how much you ate yesterday? Do you know how much you exercise on a daily basis? Do you know which of your habits are preventing you from achieving your goals?

There are so many questions that I couldn't answer about myself when I started my fitness journey. This is true for every one of us before we decide to be healthy. While we can talk about lots of root causes for why, we can't answer questions about our bodies and our habits. I think there is one main cause. For most of us, we live our lives on autopilot and are not very mindful about our health and fitness. There are so many other things that we prioritize over our own health that most of us cannot even say what we had for lunch.

Trusting your health to autopilot stops today!

When starting a project and trying to figure out the full scope of the work you are going to take on, it helps to have a full understanding of how things work today. This is often referred to as "as-is process mapping" which is essentially just walking through how things operate today and writing it down. It often means sitting side-by-side with anybody who does any work related to the things you are changing and observing what they do. Your observations include determining what information each person receives from the person before, what they do with that information, and what happens next. The goal is to write down, usually through diagrams, how things operate today so you can figure out what needs to change in order to accomplish the project goals.

Guess what? This is a very important step in your fitness project, too. Before you can build a solid plan for how you are going to achieve your goals, you need to have a full understanding of what you are and are not doing well today. By knowing what is not working today, you can determine the full scope of the changes you want to make in your new fitness routine.

Starting your fitness audit is very easy and you only need two things in order to start today — a notebook and your phone. Start with your phone and call your doctor. Make an appointment to get your annual physical or first-ever check-up as soon as you can. Ideally this appointment will include a full physical including blood work. The results from this appointment will be a critical input into your plan for how to meet your fitness goals. Also make sure to let your doctor know that you are about to start a plan.

You need a notebook because you are going to start a fitness journal. The goal of this journal is to observe and write down everything that pertains to your health and fitness for the next week or two. You want to collect enough data to give you a really good view of your habits so you can determine your true problem areas. Here are some examples of things to look for when you are doing your fitness journal.

- What is the first thing you do in the morning? Do you jump out of bed, take a shower, hit the road on the way to work and go through the drive-thru to get a breakfast sandwich on your way to the office? If so, you may immediately be ingesting more than 500 calories without thinking (and with questionable nutritional value).

- When you take that morning break and head to the coffee shop for caffeine, what do you order? Fresh brewed, black coffee is only 10 calories or less. However, some of your favorite specialty drinks may be 300-500 calories or more.

- How many alcoholic drinks are you consuming per week? Yes, you have to log your per-week number, not just your daily number. Happy hours with friends can be great, but the calories really stack up quickly with that Cosmo and a beer or two. Plus, you are more prone to eating unhealthy food with the drinks and that multiplies the effect.

- How much water did you drink through the day when you were paying attention? Be honest, was it none? Water is an important part of the fitness equation because it not only hydrates, but it also can mitigate some of the food cravings.

- What do you do when lunchtime rolls around? Do you grab food and eat at your desk or in a meeting? What kind of food are you grabbing? Are you hitting a fast food drive through again? Are you eating at a restaurant? It is pretty easy to accidentally consume an entire day's worth of calories in one meal if you aren't watching your habits.

- Most importantly, how much exercise do you get? A good way to evaluate this is the number of steps you take in a day. Smart phone users, your phone may already be monitoring this, and you don't even know it. Take a look and see how active you are. If you are getting 10,000 steps a day, that is great and you are pretty active. If you are only getting 3,000 steps a day, it may be time to take that conference call while taking a walk.

In your fitness journal, make sure to write down everything that you eat or drink throughout the day. Write down any exercise you get whether it is just normal walking around through the day or something more intentional. Make a note of your stress levels through the day and anything that is particularly frustrating. On a related note, make sure to track the number of hours you are working each day whether in the office, calls in the car, emails before and after work, or any other time you are doing work. Make a note of any pains or other ailments that you experience through the day as they may be a sign of problems that you need to address.

My fitness audit was a very eye-opening exercise that I didn't originally intend to do, but my doctor sparked my interest in doing it. During my first appointment, I couldn't answer some basic questions about my health habits. I couldn't describe a normal day of eating for him, because I didn't pay attention and had no clue about the nutritional value of my food. I couldn't tell him how many hours I was working each week, and we had to sketch it out together. I had a skewed view of how much exercise I was getting throughout the day. Plus, as I said earlier, I really didn't have the slightest clue about my weight.

As it turns out, my health and fitness conditions were much worse than I thought it was. I was getting nearly no exercise at all. I averaged 3,000 steps or so per day (thankfully, my phone was tracking this without my knowledge). I was eating high-calorie, low-nutrition foods like my daily sausage, egg and cheese breakfast sandwich from the cafeteria at work. My portion sizes were insanely oversized. I was mindlessly snacking in front of the TV and, even worse, during family game nights – if there were snacks, I was eating snacks even if I wasn't hungry. Plus, I really enjoyed craft beers, bourbon and wine and wasn't paying attention to how many drinks I was consuming.

I had no idea how many hours I was working each week and how much stress I was under. My blood pressure was a total mystery to me, and I couldn't even have guessed where it was. Similarly, I had no clue what I weighed and guessed about ten to fifteen pounds lower than what I really weighed.

The biggest ah-ha in my fitness audit was that I was operating completely mindlessly and had no idea what I was doing. I was like a fitness zombie.

Beyond everything else that I have accomplished and learned through this journey, the most important was the impact of mindlessness. Mindlessly doing anything just because it is what you have always done is the leading cause of failure in business, operations and the leading cause of poor fitness.

By simply observing your behaviors, you can quickly identify the
places where you need to take some action.

Yesterday was my 60-day mark in my commitment to diet and exercise - I am calling it "Operation Melt". In that time I am down around 40 pounds and lots of other good things. It is the only project on my plate that is going well. Really looking forward to the 50-pound mark.

OPERATION MELT
WEEK 10

Project Scope: What Will You And Won't You Do?

Once your fitness audit is complete, you will likely see things that just jump out at you that you need to change. You are probably overeating food that is not healthy for you. You may be over-drinking alcohol and sweetened beverages like soda and specialty coffees. You are likely under-exercising. Plus, there are many other potential issues that you may have found. So it is time to decide what you are going to change in order to get healthy.

The next artifact that you will need to produce in your fitness project is your project scope document or scope statement. The goal of the scope statement is to define the work, deliverables and/or activities that will, and will not, be included in your project. It is effectively the contract between the project team and the project sponsors regarding what will be done. It is used to answer the question, "What does 'done' look like in this project?" so you know when you are at the finish line. The scope statement traditionally includes the project success criteria (very much related to the charter and business case) as well as the constraints that you will be managing in the project.

If you don't know where you are going, any road will get you there.

Lewis Carroll

As you can imagine, a scope statement is a pretty important part of your fitness project in order to determine where you are going. This scope statement is the tool you are going to use to further refine your commitment to getting fit into something you can track. The scope statement is how you are going to know that you were successful.

The best place to start your scope statement is with your goal. When starting any project, it is critical to know where you are going and what you are trying to accomplish, and the more specific the better. Starting without a specific goal will reduce your probability of success.

I would recommend leveraging the SMART concept for defining your goal. SMART is an acronym that you can use to ensure that you are setting a robust goal. I have personally used two different versions of the SMART model, but they are both good. The more common model defines the attributes of a good goal as Specific, Measurable, Attainable, Realistic and Time-bound. But this version of SMART has some redundancy included in it and misses some other areas, which is why a second definition emerged. The alternate definition of SMART, which is the version I am using in this book, defines the attributes of a good goal as being Specific, Motivating, Attainable, Relevant and Trackable. As you can see both models are very similar, and you can absolutely use either one, but I have opted for the second. This means that you will want your goal to meet the following criteria.

- Specific - your goal needs to be as specific as possible in order to remove any ambiguity, so you know you have accomplished it.

- Motivating - your goal needs to be something that you are committed to achieving and can keep you motivated. You have probably already made significant progress with this with your charter and business case.

- Attainable - the goal should be something you can reach. If you choose a goal that is too aggressive, you will fail. But, make sure it is something that takes a while to reach, so you don't try to do it in one week.

- Relevant - the goal needs to be something that is relevant to you and your life versus something you will see as a "nice to have" when working on it. Again, the charter and business case set a good foundation for this.

- Trackable - finally, you need to be able to track the progress towards your goal and measure how you are doing. As I will discuss in the monitoring and controlling section, this is very important for your fitness goal and will be a big focus for you.

If you define a SMART goal when you start your journey, it will be much easier to figure out the remainder of your scope and your project plan. Plus, a good SMART goal helps keep your eyes on the prize at the end of your journey.

For example, my SMART goal for my *Operation Melt* project was to lose one-hundred pounds in less than a year in a healthy way that doesn't force me to eliminate things I like from my life, so that I am healthier and don't die an early death. This goal is certainly specific — lose one-hundred pounds in less than a year. It is motivating — be happy and don't die early is a big motivator for sure. I believed the goal to be attainable, I was far more than one-hundred pounds over my ideal weight and other people have lost that much weight, plus I was mostly confident in myself. This goal is relevant, as being significantly overweight impacts every aspect of your life. Finally, the goal is definitely trackable with just a simple scale.

So if you are losing weight, you are going to have to choose what your target weight is going to be. This is something that will require a little bit of science and may be a good place to consult with your doctor. Choosing a goal that is too low of a weight can be dangerous for your health and ultimately discouraging if you don't get there. If you choose something that isn't low enough, you will likely need to have another project to get to your healthy goal weight.

When I chose one-hundred pounds in under a year, I did so with some scientific help. I started by using my Body Mass Index (BMI) to select the one hundred pound target loss. Your Body Mass Index is a ratio of your height to your weight that is used to be a semi-universal calculation of whether you are at a healthy weight. When I first started my journey, my BMI was at 43.07 which is in the category of "obese." I decided that I want to get out of the obese category and down into the "overweight" category as a first step to improved health. When I reverse-engineered the BMI of 29.9 for me (the top of the overweight category) that translated to me needing to be one-hundred pounds lighter than I am now. Ultimately, I may want to get down to the "healthy weight" category, but that is a future goal.

Then I needed to choose the timeframe for my weight loss. I did this by doing some research on various websites and then confirming with my doctor. I researched what a healthy rate of weight loss is and I found that two pounds per week is a healthy, yet aggressive, rate of weight loss. Losing one-hundred pounds at a rate of two pounds per week translates to fifty weeks or just under one year.

So I had my goal, and my doctor agreed that it was a reasonable goal. I was all set.

Once you have determined the goal portion of your scope statement, you need to determine what you will, and will not, do to get there. This is really the heart of the scope statement because it defines the work to be done within the project. This is where you are going to need to make some decisions about how you are going to get to your goal and what you are not willing to consider.

In my project, I started by determining the things I am not open to considering. First, I was not going to adopt some fad diet or to consider surgery, so those were things that were clearly "out of scope" for my project. I had also decided that I am not willing to give up anything that I really enjoyed though I was willing to adjust quantity and frequency of indulging. I knew that I was not going to be giving up dining out because that was incompatible with my lifestyle.

Next, it is time to figure out what things are in the scope of your project. There are lots of possible options, but it really depends on what you want to do and what works for you. For my project, I included several key items in my scope statement that I was going to do to achieve my goals.

- Determine and stick to a daily calorie budget. I wanted to continually evaluate how many calories I should be ingesting every day to lose two pounds per week at my weight. Then, everything I consume within the day (food & drink) need to fit within this calorie budget.

- Increase exercise to achieve 10,000 steps per day. In addition to the diet portion of my project, I also needed to exercise more in order to burn calories. I am going to start increasing my exercise by ensuring that I hit 10,000 or more steps per day as that is often discussed as the recommended daily steps count in order to stay active. This is also a significant increase from my current level of activity.

- Increase my daily water intake. I planned to identify how much water was recommended for my height and weight and activity in order to maintain proper hydration. The popular wisdom is that consuming eight glasses of water a day (sixty-four ounces) is the recommended daily intake, but I wanted to confirm that. Then, after determining what my daily target is, I wanted to ensure I was meeting it each day.

- Reduce my weekly alcohol intake. In order to reduce calories and to generally improve my health, I decided to reduce the number of alcoholic beverages I was consuming. This includes shooting for one or two completely dry days each week and reducing what I consume on the non-dry days.

- Decrease stress and work hours. Based on the assessment I did with my doctor, it was clear that I was working an unhealthy number of hours. This was also a major driver to stress which is one of America's silent killers. So I was going to attempt to reduce how much I was working.

There you have it, this was my project scope statement for my *Operation Melt* weight loss project. This was going to be a major undertaking and was going to require some serious work and commitment. I wasn't sure how to make it all work, but that is something to figure out in the next chapter when I create my project plan. I just knew that these are the things that I needed to achieve in order to get to my goal.

Before moving on to creating our project plan, there is one other thing that you will want to think about within your scope statement. You should pause to consider the risks that may impact your ability to be successful. If you understand some of these barriers when you start your project plan, you can more proactively manage them to help yourself be more successful.

When I thought through my risks, I was able to quickly identify a few things that I was going to need to manage if I wanted any hope of success. Some of my risks may be similar to yours, or you may have way different ones in your life. It really just depends on your particular lifestyle. But ask yourself the following question and start listing out the things that come to mind:

What things may prevent me from achieving my goal?

As I mentioned above, when I thought through the risks to my journey, there were a few that were very obvious to me. Here are some of the things that I identified as risks that I needed to manage.

- I may not be able to fit exercise into my current schedule due to competing priorities.

- My job may not support me reducing my hours and stress.

- My interest or commitment to my journey may fade after a few weeks.

- I may lose track of my calories, exercise, water and such if I don't track it, and writing them down may not always be practical.

- A commitment to health and fitness is very new to me and I may not have the knowledge needed to make this project successful.

There you have it, your project scope statement is now complete. You know your goal and it is a smart goal. You know what things you will, and will not, do in order to achieve that goal. You know what risks you are going to have to manage in order to achieve success. Plus, you have a good understanding of your problem areas based on completing your fitness audit. You are now ready to build your plan for how you are going to make this happen.

When I got home for the night I happened to notice that I was 200 steps short of 20,000 total steps for the day. So I took a walk around the block just to hit that mark. Is that strange? Am I too obsessed with the numbers? I think not!

OPERATION MELT
WEEK 11

Project Plan: How And When Are You Going To Do It?

Once you have finished identifying your goal, your business case for why it is important, your items in your scope statement and your initial risks, it is time to put pen to paper again and build a plan. The next deliverable, or artifact, in your fitness project is your project plan.

A project plan is a formal document produced at the start of your project (and maintained throughout) that guides the execution of the project. Many project managers, including me, will say that the project plan is the most important artifact and tool to ensure successful delivery of your project. It is used to set and manage expectations with the project sponsors and stakeholders, it is used to measure performance of the project versus the schedule and budget, it is used to manage project risks and for many other purposes.

I like to say that the project plan tells you where you are going, how you are going to get there, when you are going to get there, all establishing the initial baseline for how you will execute your project. The project plan is then used to prove to the project stakeholders that the project is on track.

When you set out to create your project plan, you will likely spend some time staring at a blank sheet of paper (or screen) wondering where to start. It took me a weekend of contemplation before I was able to articulate my plan because it requires some serious thought to get it right, or at least to get a good start. I would suggest starting by rereading your scope statement and then thinking about what things you can do every day to make advancements in the areas you called out in your project scope. This project is going to require everyday commitment and action, so that is a good place to begin.

The second step when you create your project plan is to think a little bit more about the timeline for meeting your goal. How will you know along the way that you are on track? Start by breaking down the full goal into smaller steps that you can measure along the way. If you are planning to lose twenty-five pounds, when do you want to have lost the first five, the first ten and so forth.

Finally, when putting your project plan together, you need to think about what steps you can take to keep yourself committed. Are there certain times of the day that work better or worse for you to be active? Do you want to leverage your friends or social media as a tool to keep you accountable? Do you want to start working out with a buddy so you can motivate each other? Do you want to continue maintaining your food journal that you started during your fitness audit or start using technology? Only you really know you and that means that only you can determine the best plan to achieve your goals.

When I created my project plan, I included a few key items related to how I was going to do the things set forth in my scope statement and some incremental milestones within my journey to one hundred pounds lost. I tried to make the plan as simple as possible and there were still some unknowns that I needed to quickly figure out along the way. But I knew most of what I needed to do to get started, and I would update the plan as I got further into the journey - a concept known as rolling wave planning.

Here are the key items that I included in my project plan for my *Operation Melt* project when I first created it in June of 2017.

Start immediately! I decided that I needed to start taking action immediately rather than wait to figure everything out. I hadn't received the results of my bloodwork yet from my first doctor visit, but that wasn't going to hold me back. If I made mistakes, I would adjust later.

- Measure everything. I decided to turn toward things that have always worked for me, like project management and operations, to make this work. I guided my journey by embracing a quote from Lord Kelvin (later popularized by Peter Drucker), "If you cannot measure it, you cannot improve it." Or, said differently, if I can measure it, I can manage it. I decided to measure everything, every single day. I was going to record all of my food, all of my drinks, all of my exercise, all of my sleep, all of my work hours, my weight and anything else that mattered.

- Embrace technology. I made the decision to embrace technology to make the process easier and more fun for me - I am kind of a gadget guy.

    - I was going to find a good app (turned out to be apps) for my phone to track food and drink, and any other data.

    - I was going to invest in a wearable personal fitness tracker to monitor my exercise, heart rate, sleep, calorie burn, steps and such.

    - I was going buy a Wi-Fi connected smart scale to measure and automatically log my weight every day.

- Employ an important life hack. I have learned a lot about myself over the years and one of the important ah-has that I figured out has to do with my morning routine. The minute I get out of the shower on a weekday morning, my brain switches into work mode and I am one hundred percent focused on getting out the door. Pair this with working late and being exhausted at the end of the day, and I struggle to prioritize personal projects and pursuits. I knew that the key to my success at any personal project is to work on it first thing in the morning before taking a shower. I was going to leverage that time for my fitness project. More specifically, I was going to use my morning time as my window for exercise each day.

- Change my work hours. In order to achieve a number of my goals and to increase the morning time available for exercise, I decided to change my work hours. Instead of trying to get in the office by seven thirty or earlier each morning, I decided that I was going to arrive between eight thirty and nine each morning. This was a big change for me because I had been arriving by seven thirty or earlier for many years. But I needed to reduce my hours, create time for exercise and reduce stress, and this was how I was going to do it. I also decided I wasn't going to stay late every night either. I just needed to break all of this news to my boss.

- Exercise one step at a time. In order to increase exercise and bump up my daily step count, I started walking around the neighborhood park every morning before work. The walk to the park, one lap around and back home was about one and a quarter total miles. So I committed to walk at least one lap but wanted to target two total miles of walking before work every morning. Having an extra hour available to make this happen after changing my work schedule was going to be a big boost.

- Go public to improve accountability. I knew that I wanted to be successful with this project, and one key to that success was to talk about it. Of course, I was going to share my goal with my wife, Liz. But I was going to go beyond that and leverage my friends and social media as an accountability tool. I wanted to make sure that any failure would be a very visible failure, so I would work even harder to avoid failing.

- Prioritize myself. For the first time in many years, I decided that I was going to prioritize myself ahead of some other areas of my life. This project was very important to me, and it was going to be my first choice over other things. Becoming successful at my health and fitness was my new personal mission.

- Determine interim milestones. Finally, I laid out a set of milestones I needed to hit in order to achieve my goal of losing over one hundred pounds in under a year. The goal of these short-term milestones was to keep myself motivated by seeing progress along the way. I wasn't sure that these milestones were realistic, but I could always adjust later.

  - Lose five pounds by Fourth of July

  - Lose ten pounds before my annual vacation that started on July twenty-first

  - Lose twenty-five pounds before the Columbus Oktoberfest in September

- Lose fifty pounds by Christmas 2017

- Lose seventy-five pounds by St. Patrick's Day 2018

- Lose one hundred pounds by my one-year *Operation Melt* anniversary on June fifteenth

As I said, I tried to keep my plan pretty straightforward, yet aggressive and motivating at the same time. I was determined to make the process work and was convinced that this was the plan that was going to get me there. It turns out that the plan may not have been aggressive enough based on my results, but I did ultimately get to my goal.

My weight is an extra source of stress right now. I have exercised a ton, I have managed my calories, but my weight has gone up and not down. It is pretty frustrating to watch that happen.

OPERATION MELT
WEEK 12

Communication Plan: Who Are You Going To Tell And Involve?

Every one of us is inherently a social creature, and we are surrounded by people through many of the hours we are awake. These people could be your spouse or partner, your coworkers, your friends and other people with whom who you interact with regularly. These people are going to begin to notice changes in your behavior as you start your fitness project. Even more importantly, they are going to start seeing your results as your body starts to change. You need to think about how you want to talk about your project - to whom and when.

The final step in the project planning phase for your fitness project is the creation of your communication plan. This plan will define what you are going to say to the various groups of stakeholders (those who you interact with regularly) in the project and when you want to say it. It is likely that you are going to want to tell people about your journey at different times. These people can be very helpful allies for you and assets to help keep you focused and to make you more successful.

Start by thinking about who you want to tell about your fitness project as soon as you start it versus later.

These people should be your most trusted friends and family instead of the entire world. You will definitely want to tell your spouse or partner that you are planning to start a fitness journey. You may want to tell that person what your goal is, what your plan is and other details about your journey. You may even want to expand this audience to include your best friend(s) if that is the type of thing you talk about.

When I started my journey, I told a handful of people about my plan, my goal and why I was starting a fitness project. My initial group of people included my wife and a couple of my closest friends. Plus I had conversations with my doctor about the plan because his input and counsel was very important. These are the people who I'd relied on each day as my support system for the ups and downs of life.

The next group of stakeholders to think about when you create your communication plan would be anybody who is going to be directly or indirectly impacted. For example, I had to have a pretty direct conversation with my boss because my work schedule was going to change and she would likely see an impact. This was one of the most stressful conversations I had along the way because I wasn't sure how she was going to react. The complete list of people in this group will definitely vary based on your project plan and how you are approaching the work.

The next group that you need to consider in your communication plan is your larger network of friends and contacts. This communication will largely occur through social media and could be very beneficial to you and help with accountability. You likely won't want to immediately communicate everything to this group of people at the start of your journey and you may want to wait a bit. Plus you won't want to share all of the details of your goal, your business case, your project plan and such with this group. That information is a little more private than what you want to put in the public square that is social media.

When I started my journey, I chose not to directly say anything about it to my social network. I shared some updates along the way such as check-ins during walks and such, but I decided not to openly say that I was starting a fitness project. I waited until I had hit a major milestone in my journey before I shared the details.

The first time I openly talked about my journey on social media is when I hit my first major weight loss milestone, twenty-five pounds lost. At this point, I started telling people about my goal and what I was doing to get there. From that point forward, I continued to be more and more public about my journey and am very glad I was. It really helped me stay focused as people often asked me about how I was doing and my current status. The last thing I wanted to do was to tell my network that I quit my journey or that I gained back some of the weight.

The final consideration in your communication plan is how you are going to react when people mention your weight changes. People are going to ask you if you are losing weight and will want to know more details. You can think that it is none of their business, but they are going to ask you. Unless you just want to reply "none of your business" to their questions and compliments, you are going to want to be prepared with an answer. Be ready to respond to questions and comments such as the following.

- Are you losing weight?

- Wow, you look like you have lost weight! You look great!

- What is your secret?

- How much weight have you lost?

- Is everything ok, you look like you are losing weight?

Being prepared ahead of time with how you will be communicating about your journey will help you when that time comes. This is why the communication plan is such an important part of the planning phase for your fitness project.

Now that all of the pieces of your project plan have been defined and you know who you are going to tell about it and when, the planning phase is now complete. That is, it is complete for now, because you will continue to refine your plan as you learn more. With that, it is time to talk about execution and get this journey moving.

I am happy to report that I ran for the first time. I ran a total of about 25 feet during my walk. But, hey, that is something, right?!

OPERATION MELT
WEEK 13

Execution Phase: Let's Make This Happen!

You have a goal. You have committed to achieve it. You have built a plan for how you are going to get from where you are to where you want to be. That means you are ready to get this project moving! This is where the execution phase kicks in.

As I discussed earlier, during the execution phase, the work that was defined in your plan is performed and the real bulk of the work gets done. In a normal project, this is where the project manager plays more of a low-key role, but not in your fitness project. This is where you live your fitness journey and all of your hard work happens. This is where you have to embrace new habits and your new commitment. This is the phase where you actually build the new and improved you.

During the execution phase, you are going to be fully focused on two main factors in order to drive yourself to success: calories in and calories out. You will be diligent to ensure that what you consume every day is more than fully exhausted by the calories that your body uses.

Based on the project plan that you created, there are likely other things that need to be included in the work you do in the execution phase of your project. But, at a minimum, this is where you need to create a daily calorie deficit and start burning off the fat that makes up your extra weight.

This phase of your project is not going to be easy and will require you to sweat. But if you do it right, it will be a very productive and rewarding exercise. Plus, the better your plan, the better your results are going to be. But you will make some mistakes along the way and will need to be ready to react.

With all of that said, let's talk about how to manage your calories in and your calories out.

It has been 90 days, and my results have been really positive. I have lost 48 pounds, and I have shrunk so much that my clothes will barely stay on. Even better is that people continually give me great feedback, and I am starting to actually see my own size difference!

OPERATION MELT
WEEK 14

Calories In: Fitness Starts In The Kitchen

One of the most important decisions you will make during your fitness journey is what food and drink you will allow into your body. As you probably figured out during your fitness audit, you are eating too much of the wrong foods. Stop that now! No matter how hard you work out and no matter what other fitness decisions you make, it all comes back to the calories you choose to consume along the way, both in quantity and quality.

Let's start the discussion about calories in by talking about food. We all enjoy food, we celebrate with food, we bond over food, and it is a big part of every culture. We all remember foods as part of our memories whether it be cooking with a family member or what we were eating the day we got engaged, and so on and so forth. We romanticize food, we celebrate food, and we love food. We have certain foods that we splurge on during certain holidays, and we have foods that we use to comfort ourselves. We spend three to five hours per day focused on food between preparing and eating — that is about 35 hours per week. Food is a huge part of our lives.

I am not going to say that our relationship with food is unhealthy, but our relationship with food is unhealthy!

How much do we really need to eat?

The true reason that food exists is to fuel our bodies. We need the calories to provide the energy necessary to support our body functions and our activity. We need the nutrients for specific reasons that I can only begin to understand. It is very utilitarian for us. We could live off of an energy paste that provides the ideal balance of calories and nutrients. But that is not what we do. We enjoy our food. I am no different. I love food!

This is what gets us all into trouble. We like food so much that we over eat it, we get fat, and we die. This is why the first step to any fitness journey is to start in the kitchen. First and foremost, we need to understand what our bodies need to survive in calories and nutrients. Once we know these targets, we can make more intelligent decisions about our food choices.

Let's start with calories because that is the most important factor for weight loss. Unfortunately, the number of calories you need every day depends on a significant number of factors, many of them out of your control. Your calorie intake starts with your base metabolic rate (BMR) or the number of calories you burn at rest. Your BMR is calculated with a pretty intense mathematical equation based on your height, weight, gender and age. Your actual calorie target is also influenced by your activity level and, for women, whether you are breastfeeding or not.

Rather than providing the detailed equation to calculate your BMR I am going to make a different recommendation. Go online and find a reputable website with a BMR calculator. Alternatively you can download a good weight loss app and the calculation will be built into the app features. This is way easier than all of the nuanced math. Plus you are going to want to continually recalculate as you lose weight.

What do we need to eat?

Next you need to figure out what nutrients you need to get from your food. I would recommend not overanalyzing this and to just focus on three main areas: protein, fiber and sodium. These are the three areas where I focused, and they seemed to work well for me.

Protein is a nutrient found in both animal-based and plant-based food, (good news vegetarians!) and is used to build and maintain your muscles and tissue. You need to consume fairly large quantities of protein each day and the needs increase as your exercise levels increase. For instance, bodybuilders need a ton of protein. Protein needs increase sometimes if you are recovering from an injury or surgery because your body needs protein to rebuild itself. At a minimum, we need 0.8 grams of protein per kilogram of our body weight. The needs go up from there based on our activity levels and other factors. Based on my research, a good rule of thumb is that about ten percent to as much as thirty-five percent of our total daily calories need to come from protein.

The second nutrient that will be of interest to you in your fitness journey is dietary fiber which is sometimes called roughage. Fiber is a part of the plants that you eat in your diet. More specifically, it is the part of the plants that your body cannot actually digest. The fiber you ingest essentially passes directly through your body and back out the other end. I know that this sounds a little crazy and inefficient, but fiber is pretty important. Good sources of fiber include beans, nuts, seeds, fruits, vegetables and whole grains.

One of the primary benefits of fiber is that it helps keep you regular and keeps your bowels healthy. Regularity is surprisingly important as you start getting smaller because your body is more sensitive and may need some help. There are other benefits of fiber including helping to regulate your blood sugar and cholesterol levels — pretty important stuff. One of the most important aspects of fiber is that it helps you feel full for longer and helps minimize your cravings for food. Fewer cravings equals less eating which speeds your weight loss.

As for how much fiber you need, that also depends on the source that you believe when trying to figure it out. The most commonly quoted, referenced and most credible source that I have found for information regarding fiber intake is the Institute of Medicine. Their recommendation is that men age fifty and under target about thirty-eight grams of fiber per day and women of the same age range target twenty-five grams per day. Over fifty years old, the target drops by four grams for women and eight grams for men.

The final nutrient that I have focused on through my journey is sodium. I didn't really start paying attention to sodium until the final few months of my journey as I started experiencing its negative impacts. Sodium is a naturally occurring element in nature and is one of the two ingredients in salt (sodium and chlorine). Sodium is important to your body as we need sodium for many different biological functions including the transmission of our nerve impulses - don't interrupt that!

While sodium is important to our bodies, we don't need a lot of it. The Food and Drug Administration recommends limiting daily sodium intake to no more than 2,300 milligrams per day. The American Heart Association takes it a step further and recommends no more than 1,500 milligrams of sodium each day. Compare this to the average American's daily sodium intake of 3,400 milligrams and you see that we have an issue. The issue is that sodium is everywhere, particularly in fast food, pre-packaged foods and salty snacks. We all know that salt is a major source of seasoning in cooking and very frequently added at our dinner tables as well. Plus, sodium naturally occurs in even non-processed foods, so it is everywhere.

Overconsumption of sodium is a major risk to our health. When you consume too much sodium, your kidneys struggle to remove it from your body. As a result, your body holds onto extra water to help balance and dilute the sodium. This causes your veins and heart to work harder than they need to and causes your arteries to harden. If this goes too far, it can result in high blood pressure, heart attack and stroke. Put simply, by loading up on the salt you are killing yourself!

Beyond the risk of early death, which is a pretty big concern, there are other sodium concerns for you during your fitness journey. As I just explained, when you over-consume sodium, your body retains water as a way to dilute the sodium in your blood. Guess what? Water is not weightless and adds weight to your body. This is sometimes referred to as water weight gain or retaining water. As I got further into my journey, I began to notice significant daily weight fluctuations caused by sodium. I could accurately predict that my weight would go up, instead of down, if I had high sodium intake the day before. This could equate to putting on three or four pounds of water weight in one day, which is a frustrating moment on the scale. So to help yourself be more successful, keep an eye on the sodium intake. By doing so, you will help yourself be thinner and alive!

Finally, let's chat about water. When was the last time you had a glass of water? Is it something you do often or something you almost never do? Are you one of those people who say, "I hate the taste of water" (which is supposed to be virtually tasteless)? Well, if your relationship with water is not close, it is time to reacquaint yourself with each other and become BFFs.

Water is a critical component to healthy eating, living and fitness and you need a lot of it. Your body uses water to regulate temperature, to protect your joints from getting damaged, to clean the waste out of your body, to fuel your nervous system and to keep your skin healthy. These are important functions that you don't want to compromise, right?

In total, your body is made up of mostly water - about sixty percent. You naturally lose a portion of this water every day through sweat, breathing, going to the bathroom and so forth. You need to make sure that you are replacing the water that you lose through your diet. This includes the water absorbed from your foods, the water you drink directly and the water in other beverages. Just keep in mind that some of these other beverages, like coffee, may not be directly contributing water, and some may even be taking it away like alcohol.

We may all be familiar with the rule of thumb that we need to drink eight glasses of water a day because our body needs sixty-four ounces of water. While that is easy to remember, that may not be the right amount of water for you. In most cases, the sixty-four-ounce common knowledge will be too little water for you. Plus, if you are more active, your water needs go up even more because you are sweating more water out. Then, like everything else, your daily water intake varies based on your height and weight. For example, one recommendation I heard is that a 150 pound person needs between 75 and 150 ounces of water per day and it goes up from there. It is a big range and varies a ton, so your target may be different. There are tons of online calculators to help you figure out your daily water needs, so I would recommend getting a more specific target for yourself.

During your fitness journey, water is going to be very important to you. Your body needs it to function, so you want to take care of that! But it is also a good diet suppression tool because being full of water makes you feel full and want to eat less. Water is also a zero-calorie beverage, and you can have as much as you want without negatively impacting your daily calorie targets. Water also helps flush other calories and waste out of the body faster. Being well hydrated means that your metabolism will work faster, and your body will more quickly burn the calories that you have consumed. Finally, as I said before, you are going to be sweating more when you are exercising to burn calories, and you need to replace that lost water.

Being mindful about eating

So far, I have talked about several things that have daily consumption targets or budgets associated with them: calories, protein, fiber, sodium, water. Chances are that you have pretty much no clue how much of each of these items you are consuming today. Let me help with a guess: too much, too little, too little, too much, too little (in order). You may also be asking yourself how in the heck you are going to know how much of these you are consuming each day going forward. This brings us to the next piece of your "calories in" magic: mindfulness.

Part of how we each get overweight and unhealthy is that we don't pay close attention to what we are putting into our bodies. We operate on autopilot when it comes to foods and we just eat the things that taste good without considering what is inside them. Many food manufacturers know this, and they make sure to make the foods taste even better, and so they talk right to the parts of your mind and body that are receptive to the pleasure from foods. So you just grab whatever you want and eat as much as you want.

Unfortunately, your brain tends to let you down here and encourages you to eat too much just because it is what is on your plate or because you are eating the cookies right from the bag and there are a ton of them in there. Plus, your brain doesn't realize that you are full until long after you really are and lets you just keep eating.

My friend: this has to stop today!

From this day forward, for the rest of your life, I never want you to eat or drink one thing without pausing to consider its nutritional value. Before you order at a restaurant, I want you to think about what is contained within that dish, how many calories it has, whether it positively contributes to your nutrition and what the other options are. Before you reach into the cabinet with the snacks in it, think about it you are really hungry or just bored. Consider what food you should really eat. Before you go for seconds or dessert, pause to consider if you are really still hungry or if your brain just hasn't figured out that you are full yet. Even when you are choosing items from the salad bar, think about each item before just grabbing it. There are no freebies when it comes to food, everything has calories (kind of) and some nutrients!

I am not saying that you have to only choose the healthy options every single time by any means! You may still choose the bad food. I will often choose to eat pizza, burgers, an occasional dessert and will still have a drink or two. But I have made a decision, and I have considered the facts. I have used my brain, not just my emotions, to choose my food. I am in control of what I am doing, and I am the boss.

The difference between healthy eating and unhealthy eating is using your brain and being mindful about what you are choosing to eat. Every single thing you put in your body is a choice, and you need to choose wisely nearly one hundred percent of the time. Your fitness and your life depend on your choices.

I will take this one step further than just being aware in the moment, which is really important. I want you to commit right now to never eating or drinking another thing without writing it down. I want you to keep a food journal and write down every food, topping, side dish, drink of water, beer, tea, coffee and everything else. I want you to note the calorie content as well as the key nutrients - you can find this on the nutrition information label or, usually, on the website for the place you are eating if it is a restaurant. I want you to do this until you have reached your fitness goal.

The heart of my *Operation Melt* fitness project was to capture every data point every time and to ensure that they are within my goals. I didn't hit my goals one hundred percent of the time, but I could look back and know what decision(s) I made that caused me to miss the target. I wouldn't beat myself up about them, but I would be aware. Then, very early in my journey, I started making decisions based on where I was versus my targets instead of just looking backwards and adding things up that I already ate. It is a lot like making household spending decisions based on a monthly budget instead of just buying anything you want. It matters, and it is the difference between delivering this project as planned or killing it part way through.

Will you commit to being mindful about your consumption and to staying within your calorie and nutrient budgets every day?

How to choose your foods

Being mindful about what you are consuming every day doesn't mean that you can't eat and can't eat well. On the contrary, you are going to be able to eat a lot of a great variety of foods every day. You are even going to be able to, and you absolutely should, still eat the things you enjoy and even still enjoy alcohol. You will just need to do it in moderation and seek out good, clean foods. Here are some suggestions about how to make it work.

First, think about the structure of the meals that you eat today. What percentage of your plate is dedicated to meat, starch and vegetables? This is an easy thing to change to help focus on the right way to eat to support your journey. Start off by adjusting the proportions of foods on your plate so you have at least fifty percent of your plate dedicated to fruits and vegetables with a heavy focus on the vegetables. The more you shift your diet to plant-based foods, the easier it will be to control your calorie intake, your fiber and your sodium. Then, limit the meat portion of your meal to twenty-five percent or so of your plate. As you train harder and harder, you may need to ramp this up a little bit so you are getting enough protein. The last twenty-five percent of your plate can be starches and dairy, if you so desire, or more vegetables. This is not an exact formula by any means, but it is a directional recommendation instead of the way you are likely doing things today. But, since you are tracking everything you are eating, you will be able to adjust properly to ensure you are getting the nutrients that you need.

Increasing your intake of vegetables is a big first step to increasing the amount of "clean" foods that you eat. When I say "clean," I mean limiting the foods that you eat that are processed and pre-packaged. Focusing on fresh, natural foods with minimal preservatives and other added ingredients is a recipe for success in your fitness journey.

Read the ingredient labels on the foods you are eating and make sure that they still sound like something you want to put into your mouth during this journey.

While you are reading the label on your foods, make sure to also read the nutritional facts on the label. Pay close attention to the serving size, the calories, the fat, the sodium, the vitamins, the protein and the fiber. Make sure that you understand the composition of the foods and whether it contributes to, or detracts from, your fitness goals. Again, it is about being mindful and making good decisions.

The next thing to focus on regarding the foods that you choose to consume is how the foods are prepared. Some preparations are healthier than others, and there are some that you are going to want to avoid where possible. As you may expect, deep fried foods are near the top of the list of ones to minimize or avoid completely. But, creamy and rich foods like Alfredo sauces and foods smothered in melted cheese are other calorie bombs that can easily side-track your nutrition goals. Conversely, simply grilled meats and vegetables tend to be much healthier than other preparations of the same things. When you are at a restaurant, don't be afraid to ask questions about how the foods are prepared if you don't know.

Next, pay close attention to the side dishes, appetizers, accompaniments and post-meal add-ons. All of these secondary pieces of your meal pile on the calories. For example, the basket of bread may be one hundred calories per piece, and the butter adds to that. The appetizer can be worse off than the main course, and then you throw a dessert on top of that. Plus, with sandwiches, the bread or bun may be more calories than what is in between. Then, there are the condiments such as mayo and aioli that are also calorie surprises.

Finally, you should use your new commitment to fitness and mindfulness as an opportunity to try new things. Through my journey, I learned that I loved a variety of things that I would not have previously chosen. For example, avocado toast, overnight oats, tofu, quinoa, octopus and many other things are new adds to my diet that weren't there before. Plus, I make my own foods more and choose better restaurants. But, I did not fully eliminate anything from my diet along the way, especially the things I enjoy. I just manage how much I eat of everything instead of trying to eliminate things like pizza and beer from my diet.

> *Reflecting on this week I can't help but to be a little disappointed in my progress. But I need to just accept it. So I missed my expected 50-pound loss milestone this week. I will achieve that by next week, and it will be just as special.*

OPERATION MELT
WEEK 15

Calories Out: You Have To Get Moving

The foods that you consume are a very important foundation of your fitness journey, but there is another piece that is equally important: calories out. You are going to need to ensure that you have enough physical activity to burn off the calories you consume and some additional calories in order to burn the fat that you are carrying around. This is where exercise comes into the picture. I am not saying that you need to instantly become an athlete, but you are going to need to get moving in order to get melting!

Safety First!

The exercise part of your journey is an area where you need to be careful and focus on your safety. It is very easy to jump into an exercise routine and attempt to do too much, too fast and end up injuring yourself. With any exercise routine, the trick is to start slow and ramp up as your skills permit. If you start feeling pain, rest that part of your body and don't try to push through it or you may be sidelined for a while. Like anything, if you are in doubt about your abilities, pain you are experiencing or anything else, please seek professional input from a doctor or other knowledgeable source. I caution you from trying to self-diagnose any medical condition through Internet searches. That could be a costly mistake.

Types of Exercise

With the safety warning out of the way, let's start with a quick discussion about the multiple types of exercise that you will want to draw from during your journey. I am just going to review at a high level, but you will want to continue learning more as you progress.

The first, and I would argue most important type, of exercise you will need to add to your routine is cardio (short for cardiovascular) which is also known as aerobic exercise. This type of exercise involves getting enough physical activity to get your heart rate to increase and your breathing to get more rapid. By elevating your heart rate and breathing, your body will burn more calories than it does at rest. Some of the exercises in this category include walking, running, cycling, swimming and anything else that gets you moving.

Cardio will be the primary, but not only, exercise you will want to use to help get your body to start burning those calories. There are many different recommendations for how much cardio exercise we each need, but one commonly cited one comes from the *American College of Sports Medicine*. They recommend either thirty minutes of moderate cardio exercise five times per week or twenty minutes of intense cardio three times per week. But this recommendation is intended for maintaining weight. If you are trying to lose weight, you will need more. We will talk more about how to get that exercise in a bit.

The second type of exercise that you eventually will need to add to your life is weight training also known as strength conditioning. This form of exercise involves repetitive motions with some form of resistance and is intended to work your muscles to ultimately make them grow and make you stronger. The form of resistance you use during weight training can vary and may include free weights (barbells, dumbbells), weight machines, resistance bands or simply body weight. For example, push-ups are a form of weight training that only uses your body weight.

Again, recommendations for frequency of strength training tend to vary. One common recommendation that I often hear is to do strength training at least twice a week but not every day. Weight training every day does not give your muscles enough time to recover in between sessions and will ultimately limit the effectiveness of the weight training. It is especially important not to do strength training for the same body part for multiple consecutive days.

When you are doing weight training, focus on reps (repetitions) and sets for each exercise. The reps are the number of consecutive times you lift the weight or do the exercise without stopping between. Sets are the number of times you repeat a group of reps. For each exercise, target completing ten to twelve reps, then resting and then repeat. It is typical to do this two or three times, or two or three sets of ten to twelve reps.

Weight training, if not done properly, comes with a higher risk of injury, but it is pretty easy to manage that risk. First, be careful not to overdo it with the amount of weight that you are lifting. Start with something comfortable and gradually ramp up as your body allows. Also, pay close attention to your form when you are training and ensure that you are using smooth, fluid motions, not moving too fast. Finally, don't drop weights onto your hand, foot, head or really any body part of your own or one that belongs to somebody else.

The third type of exercise that I want to talk briefly about is stretching or flexibility training. The goal of stretching is to engage and flex your muscles with gentle motions to gradually improve their elasticity. This is important because stretching will help, not just your flexibility, but it will also help you prepare for, or recover from, other exercises. Stretching will help prevent injury and pain, and will ultimately make you perform better. Just be careful not to stretch your muscles too much or in a non-natural manner or else you might hurt yourself.

It is important not to try to aggressively stretch muscles that are cold. This really applies to any form of exercise that you are doing. If you just jump in and push yourself hard when your muscles aren't ready, you can hurt yourself. This is why the concept of warm-up exercises is so important. You get your body moving and flexing in a gentle way before pushing yourself to work harder. Warm-up exercises get the blood flowing through your body and into your muscles which, in turn, makes them warmer and more flexible so you can work them harder without hurting yourself. A slow walk for a few minutes is a good way to get your muscles warmed up and ready to go.

You need to start small

I am sure that you have probably heard the famous quote from Lao Tzu, "The journey of a thousand miles begins with a single step." Essentially, he is saying to start small and that will get you to your goal. This same concept certainly applies to exercise. Start with something that is comfortable, that won't discourage or frustrate you, and something that won't cause you pain. If you start there, you can ramp up as time goes on. This is how success is built!

When I started my journey, I chose an easy exercise to get started, walking. In the mornings, before I got ready for work, I went out for a comfortable walk around the park in my neighborhood. From my house to the park, one lap around the park and then back home was a total distance of about one and a quarter mile. At my initial pace, I could finish this walk in under thirty minutes and it would burn about 250 calories or so. Eventually, I increased my pace a bit and ultimately extended the distance to two total miles. It wasn't a strenuous workout at all, but it was enough to start adding more exercise into my life and caused me to burn some calories.

Eventually, my body started becoming healthier and the walking became a less effective form of exercise. Essentially, this means that the same pace and distance wasn't causing as much elevation in my heart rate and breathing, and as a result, it wasn't burning as many calories. I had to increase the distance to get the same calorie burn, but that also meant adding more time to my walk. I chose to start increasing the pace and mixing in a little bit of running into the walking. It took me about two months before I started adding running into my exercise routine and I would only run about twenty-five feet in a mile-long walk at first. But, by the seven-month mark, I could actually run a full mile.

There was no way that I could have started on the first day of my journey by running a mile. At the worst, it could have been dangerous to suddenly ramp up my physical activity that much. At best, it would have been uncomfortable and frustrating when I couldn't do it and may have caused me to quit. But, I started with one step.

In addition to the morning walks, I began walking instead of driving for short trips in my neighborhood. I also tried to insert more walking into my daily activities by parking further away from the office, taking breaks through the day to take a walk and other similar approaches to increasing my distance. Every little bit of physical activity adds up to big impacts to your health and fitness.

Once October rolled around, the weather started getting a bit colder in Columbus, so I needed to think about taking my exercise game indoors. This is when I decided to join a gym in the neighborhood, so I could continue my walking (and running) on their treadmills. Plus, joining a gym meant that I had more access to other equipment such as weights and weight machines, so I could start adding in weight training. Ultimately, the gym became kind of addictive. I craved going there as frequently as possible, but it wasn't every day.

I am telling you the story of when I joined the gym to make an important point about starting small. I joined the gym almost five months into my journey. Before then, I didn't need to spend money, use fancy machines or even really do weight training in order to get exercise and see impressive results. The only equipment I needed to get started was a good pair of athletic shoes and the will to get started and keep going. I would also recommend using your phone and earbuds so you can add some music or an audiobook to help keep you entertained, but don't forget to pay attention to the nature and sights around you, too. For the first month of my journey, I may not have even really broken a sweat and the exercise wasn't hard, painful or discouraging. Plus, the exercise was a way of relieving the stress that I was experiencing from a highly demanding job.

My initial exercise goal when I started was very basic, walk 10,000 steps per day versus the 3,000 I was averaging until that point. I didn't get to my goal every day and rarely achieved it at first. But I kept focused, and it became easier and easier to get there. In the later stages of my first phase of *Operation Melt*, there were days when I achieved the 10,000 steps before breakfast. But, there are still days where I don't reach 10,000 and there are some rare days where I don't even get half of that. But it is an everyday goal, and I keep trying.

In your journey, choose something that is easy for you to do in order to get started. It could be walking, it could be swimming, it could be cycling or anything else that you enjoy and is easy for you to do. Then keep doing it until you are ready to do more, then do more.

Make it a habit

By now, I think you can tell that exercise isn't something that you are just going to do one time, it is something that you need to do daily. For each of us, it is far easier to achieve something every day if we build a routine and make it a habit. You reach a point where you no longer have to make a choice regarding whether or not you do something, it just becomes your routine. Your goal should be to get to this stage with exercise. Make it a routine and a habit that you don't have to actively choose whether to do it or not. The more you remove the moment of choice and just assume the choice is yes, the more likely you will be to stick with it.

Unfortunately, it is going to take some time before you get into a routine and make your exercise a habit. Be deliberate and focused in order to get the ball rolling. This means that getting started with an exercise routine will require some willpower. There are other things you could be doing that, at first, that you enjoy more. Odds are, this is why you haven't started an exercise routine before today. So when you get started, find the time when your willpower is highest and when you have the most ownership of your time so you are least likely to get distracted. You will know best what this means for your life, but I will tell you that for most people, it means the mornings.

First thing in the morning is usually the best time to insert exercise into your day. You may not be a morning person, but this may be the time to adjust some of those habits. First, our willpower, self-control and discipline is usually highest in the morning. As you go through the day, all of the events and stressors of the day tend to drain your willpower reserves. So as you get later in the day, you are less likely to be able to stick with your routine. Also, if your work day is like mine, the end of your day becomes far less predictable. I may try to leave the office at 5:00, but that time may get pushed to 6:00, 6:30 or later, and then I am ready for dinner. So, inserting exercise at the end of the day would have increased the probability that I would decide to skip it. Lastly, the morning is usually the easiest time for you to create more time in your schedule if needed. Set your alarm earlier and get out of bed ready to go.

No matter how you get yourself started, it is important to get moving with your exercise routine so you can make it a habit. Then, after you have made it a habit, your next step is to make it a passion or mission!

Mix it up and try new things

If you do exactly the same thing every single day in any area of your life, you get into more than a habit, you get into a rut. Just think about going out to dinner. If you went to the exact same restaurant and ate the exact same dish every day, you would get pretty bored. The same thing applies to your exercise routine. When you get into a rut, you get bored and you find reasons to stop working out.

There is an easy way to avoid getting bored with your exercise routine and that is by continually trying new things. Something as simple as changing up your walking route a few times each week can keep things interesting and keep you coming back each day. Other ways to mix it up could be to try new exercises, take a class or try a preset workout routine. Find ways to make tomorrow's exercise different from today's exercise.

One of the first ways that I mixed up my routine was by changing where I was walking. In the April through October timeframe, my wife and I split our time between Columbus and Indian Lake, a small community just an hour away. By default, this gave me the opportunity to walk in two very different towns. Plus, I would choose alternate locations in each town as the location for my walks, though I would usually walk around the park in my Columbus neighborhood during the week. But a nice long walk along the lake, on a trail or elsewhere provides a change of scenery.

I also started mixing up the type of exercise I was doing. As I already mentioned, I started adding some running into my daily walking as I started getting more fit. This became a good way to add variety and to challenge myself. I would start out with a walk from my house to the park, which is a good warm-up, and then I would run as far as I could until I was exhausted and needed to slow to a walk. I noticed my running distance increase over time and that kept me interested. Plus, when I joined my gym, I was able to mix in weight training and other exercises. I even took a yoga class and loved it.

Mixing up your exercise routine is good for a number of reasons. First, it keeps it interesting and keeps you from getting bored with exercise. This is a good way to keep you committed and coming back every day. But, there is another good reason for mixing up your routine, your body needs it. You are going to get better and better as you progress through your journey and the same exercises are not going to be as effective. If you don't mix up your exercises, you are going to see your results start to trail off. If your results start to decline, you will get discouraged and are more likely to quit.

Set goals, crush them, set bigger goals

My final note on "calories out" and the execution phase is about goals and measurement. As I have said over and over, part of how *Operation Melt* was successful is that I measured and tracked everything I did along the way. I knew every calorie in and every calorie out and that is an important thing for you in order to help achieve your goals. So in addition to keeping a food journal, keep an exercise journal too.

Every time you exercise, note it in an exercise journal along with how many calories you burned during the exercise. Note how many steps you take every day using a pedometer or the capability built into your phone. Make notes of how you felt during the exercise and how much you are improving. Note it all, and you will be able to figure out what is most important.

Not only will tracking every piece of information about your exercise help you remember what you have done, but it will help in another way too. By having data, you can start setting smaller goals every day or week. For example, if you have only been averaging 8,000 steps per day for the past two weeks, you can challenge yourself to 9,000 steps next week. If you were able to bench press twenty pounds last week, how about trying twenty-five pounds this week. By having the data, you can set goals and then see how you performed versus those goals. This is the way to help you feel like you are winning every day.

As you are progressing through your exercise journey, set some goals every week and then try to crush them. Don't just get to your goal, blow right past it and really push yourself (safely) to accomplish big things. Once you achieve something big, reward yourself with a bigger goal and repeat the process.

When I first started running, I could only run for about one half of one side of the park in my neighborhood - that is one-eighth for you fraction fans. By the time it started getting too cold to run outside, I had reached the point where I could run around one full side of the park and about halfway around side two — three-eighths total. I set a goal that I wanted to be able to run one full lap around the park by spring. In the meantime, I was running and walking on the treadmill in the gym. Then, in early February there was a warm week in Columbus, and I could run outside. Just a quick note here, when I say "run," I really mean a lot of walking with some running patches inserted. I still walk fair amount when I am running. But, back to my story... The first time I ran outside, I wanted to achieve my goal of running a full lap around the park and I crushed that goal. I ran three full laps totaling two full miles of running without having to slow to a walk. It wasn't easy, but I did it. That is when I decided I need to add another lap to get to two and a half miles. I realized that I can build up to being able to complete a 5k race.

I want to address one more part of the process when it comes to exercise, pain. When you are pushing yourself harder and harder to achieve your goals, your muscles are going to be performing in ways that they don't usually perform. The way your muscles grow is by effectively tearing and rebuilding after your workouts. You are undoubtedly going to experience some mild pain along the way. Notice that I said "mild" pain not excessive or excruciating pain, that is very bad. But, mild pain is normal and is actually healthy. For example, the first time that I decided to add lunges and squats to my workout routine resulted in pain the next day. It hurt to sit down, it hurt to walk down stairs, but that pain actually made me grimace and smile at the same time. I knew that I had accomplished something new. I was happy that I felt the pain because I knew I had worked out hard. You don't want pain every single day, but when you try something new and you go at it hard, it is ok to feel some soreness the next day.

By starting small with your exercise and ramping up, you will be amazed by how far you can progress in your fitness journey. Then by mixing up the exercises, you can keep yourself motivated for long enough that you can make exercise a habit and then a passion. If you keep track of all of your exercise and calories out, you will be able to start setting incremental exercise goals for yourself, so you can push yourself to keep improving. That everyday success and improvement until you reach your goal is the heart of what the execution phase of your fitness project is all about.

I did it. I have lost more than 50 pounds in 100 days! Since I started this fitness journey, I have lost 51.4 pounds! Plus I am feeling better and have even started running a little bit - that is something that was unthinkable to me in the spring!

OPERATION MELT
WEEK 16

Monitoring & Controlling Phase: Staying The Course

As I mentioned earlier in this book, the monitoring and controlling phase happens in parallel with the execution phase of your project. The goal of this phase is for the project manager to track the project and react as needed. The goal is to make this a very fact-based phase and to track the progress based on a set of defined measurements or key performance indicators (KPIs). If the KPIs indicate that the project is deviating from the plan, corrective action may be required in some form.

The monitoring and controlling phase is equally as important in your fitness project as it is in any other project. The goal is to track your progress both proactively and reactively, and to continue to take the necessary steps to stay on track. This phase is the one that separates successful fitness projects from the ones that fail - the vast majority of fitness projects.

In my *Operation Melt* project, this was probably the most important phase for me. I tend to be a very numbers-driven person in projects and in operational areas for which I am responsible. The numbers are how I determine if I am on track, or if I am ahead or behind in my plan.

Numbers are empirical measurements of facts and always tell the truth. Yes, it is possible to lie with numbers and people do all the time, but that is an intentional skewing of facts. Numbers are also big motivators for me and are how I stay focused on the goal.

Whatever you do in your fitness project, please do not overlook the importance of the monitoring and controlling phase. If you do, your success in your journey will be purely coincidental and not managed as a project. In which case, you wasted a ton of time reading this book.

*My reward for hitting the
50-pound mark was taking a day
off work just for myself called
"Tony Day." I used the day to go
clothes shopping, and I can
finally say goodbye to the big &
tall store. This is something I
didn't expect to be able to do in
my life.*

OPERATION MELT
WEEK 17

Motivation: Stay Committed, Stay Focused, You Will Win!

In any long project, one of the most important things that you can do as a project manager is to inspire, recognize and motivate your team so they stay focused. You want the team to continually recommit to the goal, to enjoy the journey and to feel successful along the way. If your team doesn't feel engaged, they won't do their best work, and the project might fail. This is absolutely needed in your fitness project too.

In your fitness project, you have set a big and important goal for yourself, and you aren't going to be able to get there tomorrow. This project is going to take some time. So, you need to continue to fuel your motivation in order to stay committed. If you don't, you are going to get bored, you are going to lose interest, and you aren't going to win. You didn't start this journey to fail, and I want you to be successful. So let's talk for a second about motivation.

There are lots of ways that you get motivated and you are going to need to draw from all of those different options to keep this journey going. I talked about this a little bit through the chapters in the execution section when I discussed mixing up your exercises, setting smaller goals, trying new foods and choosing the right time of the day to exercise. But, there are a wide variety of other things you can do to stay motivated. These other options fall into two main approaches: self-motivation (where you are motivating yourself) and social motivation (where your motivation is being influenced by others).

Self-Motivation

First, as is the basic premise of this book, set a specific goal with a motivating reason behind it and track your progress every single day. The goal and progress tracking will set the stage for keeping you motivated. If you are a numbers-driven person, and most project managers definitely are, seeing the numbers change will be a huge motivator for you. This is good because the numbers will change faster than the visible changes to your body, so you are going to see the results quickly. This can be bad also because there will be times where the numbers don't go the way you want or don't move at all, and you don't want your commitment to fall apart. So you are going to need something beyond the numbers, something more emotional.

Next, there is the music you listen to while working out. You know there are some songs you listen to and you just feel yourself getting motivated. You may feel your heart rate increase when the song comes on and you may feel your energy go up. Note what these songs are and find more of them. Create a playlist on your phone or other device to listen to in order to get yourself motivated.

When it comes to getting motivation from music, I have two different types of motivation playlists. First is a "pump-up" playlist. These are the songs that you hear that make your heart rate increase, that put you into a powerful mood and remind you that it is time to be fierce. These are usually powerful, hard-driving songs that vary based on your musical tastes, but I find hip hop and hard rock to be good here. The goal of this type of playlist is to get you motivated to start moving so you are unstoppable.

The second type is an "endurance" playlist to listen to on longer walks, runs or whatever cardio you do. These are the songs that you are going to enjoy hearing for a longer period of time, and that put you into the "zone." You may find that you ultimately forget that you are even exercising. This could even be a good time for you to insert audiobooks if that is what does it for you.

Another source of motivation is online videos. Video streaming services have tons of content that can work as both pump-up and endurance motivators. On some treadmills, you can even watch TV, movies (a new, healthier way to binge watch, right?) or access online videos right from the treadmill to keep you in the zone for longer periods of time. Early in my journey, I found one video on an online service that took soundbites from super motivational speeches or movies and overplayed them on a hard-driving soundtrack. When I watch or even just listen to this video, I am a force to be reckoned with and unstoppable. I feel my heart rate increase and I feel like I have to move. I reach peak levels of performance just because this is playing in the background. It is kind of amazing!

Next up in our list of motivators are the affirmations and Internet memes. These short quotes and cool pictures are made to motivate you. One of my favorite examples of these types of motivators are quotes from legendary boxer Muhammad Ali. He was amazing at the self-affirming quotes, and we could all learn some things from him. One great and affirming quote of his that I like is, "I am the greatest. I said that even before I knew I was."

Find a few quotes and affirmations to reread on a regular basis and that you can say to yourself. Don't be afraid to say them out loud. Look for things that you can use to motivate yourself and remind you of how powerful you are. There are tons of them, and I have found that the really do work for me.

While you are surfing the Internet looking for inspirational quotes, memes, videos and music, there is a final form of self-motivation you can find out there, immersion. One key thing that has worked to help me maintain my motivation is by immersing myself in the health and fitness world. I follow people on social media, read articles every day and learn from other peoples' stories that they have shared. In short, I try to learn more every day. By learning more, I get ideas of new things to try and find new ways of looking at my journey. I also can see where I have progressed in my journey versus where other people are in theirs. By continually immersing myself in information sources surrounding health and fitness, it becomes a mental pursuit for me. Health and fitness has become a part of who I am, not just what I do, and that creates a motivation snowball of sorts that keeps getting bigger the further it progresses.

Social Motivation

So far, I have talked about several mechanisms for self-motivation, but we are also social creatures and don't have to go it alone. There are lots of ways that we can leverage other people to help provide some of the motivation we need to stay the course. The goal is effectively to leverage peer pressure to help keep you from straying from your goal. One easy mechanism for this is one that you will get for free along your journey. As you progress and start showing visible results, people will definitely start to notice even before you do. Some people aren't shy and won't hesitate to speak up about what they see. You will get positive feedback and, once you get past the initial awkwardness of somebody telling you that you look good because you aren't as fat, you will want more!

The second way to leverage social motivation is through social media. If you have decided to go public with your journey instead of keeping it quiet, social media can be an invaluable resource for you. Post pictures as you change, check-ins at the gym, results from workouts, weight loss milestones and other updates along the way. People like to read these positive updates about your success, and you will get lots of likes and comments. Don't hesitate to use social media as a great tool to keep yourself accountable and to keep yourself motivated. Just don't overdo it with the sharing or people will start to unfriend you because you are annoying. Try to find a healthy balance.

Another way that you can leverage others is by finding some buddies, even just one person, who you can work out with. This could be a running group, a trainer, friends or just people you meet at the gym. By committing to work out together, you will instantly be more accountable to getting to your workout. People will notice when you aren't there, and you won't want to let them down. It is always easier to stay committed when somebody is doing it with you.

In early March, at a point when I had lost ninety-seven pounds, I made a decision to go to the *2018 Arnold Sports Festival* for the first time in my life. Arnold Schwarzenegger's multi-sport festival and exposition of all things fitness has been held in Columbus for thirty years. I never had the urge to ever go before, but this year I wanted to be there. One big reason I wanted to go to this event was to gain social motivation by surrounding myself with experts. At this event, I got to watch hundreds of amateur athletes participating in their craft. Most, or all, of these people are way ahead of me in their journeys, and there is a lot that I could learn from them. Plus, watching these people compete made me work way harder the next morning at the gym. Very motivational!

Surrounding yourself with experts doesn't have to mean real experts, per se. Seeking out your friends who are ahead of you in their fitness also works. I have lots of friends who are runners or other fitness enthusiasts, and I talk to them often about my journey. I have learned a lot from these people, and it has helped me get better. For example, I was discussing a treadmill workout with one of my friends and learned that part of why my duration wasn't improving is that I was running a bit too fast. This helped me perform better in my very next workout. Plus, this is one more way to immerse yourself in your journey because you are talking about it with others. Talking about your journey is the basis for my last motivation tool.

My last suggestion for how to stay focused and motivated is something that I am doing right now, telling your story. Yes, posting on social media tells bits of your story, but find other outlets to share. Tell people what you have learned, and help them be successful in their journey as well. That is why I started my blog on *OperationMelt.com* as I got into my journey. I wanted to help other people because inspiring others to start their own successful journeys paid big dividends in my own motivation and made me want to stay ahead of them to keep helping. Telling your story and praising yourself for your accomplishments can be a critical tool to helping yourself and others accomplish big goals.

I went very public with my journey and told lots of people that I was doing it. In addition to keeping me positively motivated, this created a big consequence if I failed. All of these people would know I failed, and I would fall hard if I fell. This is the kind of thing that I needed to help me stay motivated. You may not want to do it exactly the same way, but it worked well for me.

This week I had my first 1000-plus calorie loss workout and my best run yet! Both were big milestones in my journey and big wins for me!

OPERATION MELT
WEEK 18

Progress Tracking: Monitoring Your KPIs

Earlier in this book, I explained that the core premise of my *Operation Melt* fitness project was a quote that essentially says, "If I can measure it, I can manage it." Put simply, the things that can be converted into empirical measurements can be monitored, goals can be set and improvements can be implemented to change the metrics. So for my fitness project, I chose to measure everything related to my body and to continue to manage my journey based on those measurements. This was a very successful approach for me and is the approach I would recommend for anybody who wants to use project management as their way to better health.

I often say that I measured everything during my journey, but that is a little bit of hyperbole. I didn't measure *everything* I could have, but I measured a lot of things. I measured a variety of data related to nutrition and consumption, data related to activity and calories burned, my weight and the vital signs in my body. I measured these things every single day and reacted to what the data told me. But, in full transparency, I over-measured both in terms of the data and the frequency. This worked out well for me because I was able to look back and learn what was, and was not, important data for my journey, and I was able to refine my plan to focus on the most important things.

In fitness, there are nearly countless data points that you can measure to give you an indication of your progress on a daily basis. The trick is measuring a small number of critical metrics. Otherwise you are going to be spending all of your time measuring and much less working.

As I discussed in the chapters related to the execution phase, you must keep a journal to track data regarding the foods that you consume (calories and nutrients,) as well as the exercises that you engage in. This helps you get to your calories in and calories out measurements. There are also a variety of other measurements that also help you know how you are performing.

The KPIs that I have used to track progress in my *Operation Melt* project fall into two major categories: the important and the interesting. Important KPIs are those that will be the best indication (either predictor or measurement) of your progress, and the interesting KPIs are also good indicators, but are more nice-to-have measurements. Note that the interesting KPIs are a lot harder to track without help from other tools.

Let's start with the *important* KPIs because they are, well... important. For each of these KPIs, I track the data daily, and set targets and budgets on a regular basis against which I measure my progress. Each one of these measurements is either a "leading" indicator because it predicts future results or a "lagging" indicator because it is a result on its own.

- **Weight:** I measure my weight every day to monitor progress. Yes, there are daily fluctuations up and down. Yes, it can be maddening, but this is the overall result I am trying to influence, so I need to measure it. Weight is an example of a lagging KPI because it is a result and not something you can control in the moment.

- **Calorie Intake:** This is where your food journal comes into the picture. I measure and record everything that I consume, whether it be food or drink, and log the calories as well as key nutritional information (protein, fiber, sodium, etc.). I compare this to my daily calorie target which is determined based on my height, age, gender and current weight. Just for some perspective, my daily calorie target is usually set just under my base metabolic rate, the number of calories my body will naturally burn at rest. Calorie intake is an example of a leading KPI because it helps predict what will happen with my weight in the future.

- **Nutrients:** Late in my *Operation Melt* journey (around 90 pounds lost), I started paying more attention to the nutrients in my food and not just calories. I was particularly interested in ensuring I got enough protein and fiber while minimizing salt. I had specific targets for each of these based on my age, height, weight and activity levels.

- **Step Count:** I measure total steps taken each day and my goal is to stay at 10,000 or more steps. I like step count because it is a good indicator of overall physical activity for a day and I can impact it at a moment's notice. Plus, I can set hourly step targets to build to the daily target which makes it an instant motivator.

- **Exercise Calories:** I track the calories that I burn during specific workout activities, usually walking or running. Be careful not to just blindly trust measurements from treadmills and exercise equipment which don't factor in your height and weight. These are just averages that aren't necessarily true for you.

- **Net Calories:** In addition to measuring calories I ingest, I also measure net calories after factoring in the calories burnt during specific exercise times and workouts. My calculation is Base Calorie Budget minus Calories from Food and Drink plus Exercise Calories equals net calories for the day.

- **Water Intake:** I log all water I drink or any other non-alcoholic fluid intake. I exclude alcohol because it is actually dehydrating. I compare to a daily target that I set based on research related to my height, weight, gender and activity level.

Those are the most important KPIs that I track every day which are the ones that are the best indications of how I am progressing against my goal. If you don't measure anything else, measure those and ensure that you are meeting your goals every day and are creating a calorie deficit. If so, you should see your weight generally decreasing on average, just not every day.

I mentioned that there are additional KPIs I track that I refer to as "interesting" KPIs that aren't as important. These KPIs are indicators of my overall health and wellness, but aren't as directly impactful to my goal. If you choose to track these too, make sure not to spend as much time on them as you do on the important KPIs.

- **Distance Walked:** This KPI is very closely tied to steps is the total distance you walked. It is not critical to measure both, but I use it as a good motivator. I try to walk about five miles per day (which is about 10,000 steps for me). It is sometimes fun to figure out what your walking distances translate to in geographic terms. For example, in the first five months of my *Operation Melt* project I walked 736 total miles which is the entire length of Italy.

- **Active Minutes:** I track how many minutes each day that I spend doing physical activity, usually activity that lasts more than ten minutes. My goal is to exceed the *American College of Sports Medicine* recommendation of twenty minutes per day for five days per week. I try to hit thirty minutes or more every day.

- **Sleep Hours:** I track how many hours I actually sleep each day. I know that I should get eight hours of sleep per day and am usually nowhere close. Sleep is very important to rejuvenate you each day and to keep your mind focused.

- **Resting Heart Rate:** I track my resting heart rate each day because it is a good indicator of my overall state of fitness and stress. When I first started my journey, my resting heart rate started in the seventies and it had fallen to the mid-fifties by the time I reached my goal. This means that my heart doesn't have to work as hard to keep my body functioning which is good in the long run.

- **Total Calories Burnt:** I also track the total calories I burnt each day including my base metabolic rate and my active calories. This is important because one pound of weight loss translates to about 3,500 calories burnt above those consumed.

Rely on Technology

I clearly tracked a ton of data through my journey, but I didn't do this without the help of some important technology. While you could track many of these data points by hand through your food journal and some Internet time, that isn't the easiest way to do it. Plus, my entire career (and big portion of my life) has revolved around technology in some manner. As such, I am a firm believer that an important factor that contributes to project management effectiveness is to employ technology as an aide to achieve your goals.

Trying to accomplish big things without the assistance of the appropriate technology makes the journey harder than it needs to be. Can you imagine how hard it would be to manage a huge, multiyear, multimillion dollar project without systems and tools? You would have to do it manually via pen and paper, and operational efficiency would be impossible. Similarly, when you consider all of the KPIs I mentioned above, it would be nearly impossible to measure them without support from the right technology.

I will share the technology tools that I used, but I am not going to talk about specific brands for each item. There are a ton of options out there and many of them are very good, so I don't want to sway you one way or the other. Plus, while I chose some specific apps and tools for my *Operation Melt* project, I am not sure that I used all the best options. These options just worked well for me, and I hesitated to switch once I started.

- **Smart Phone:** I use my phone (and tablet) as the key hub of all of my KPI tracking and fitness. Every tool I use has an app associated with it, and I can view all of my metrics at a glance just from my phone.

- **Food Tracker App:** I use an app on my phone to log all of the food and beverages I consume. This app has a massive food database where I can find most things that I consume or add custom entries when I have something new. The app tracks calories and nutrients, and I can also record all of the calories I burn from exercise each day in this app in order get to my net calories for the day.

- **Water Tracker App:** I use a separate app to track hydration. My food-tracking app can also track water, but I didn't like the way it functioned. So, I chose a standalone app to log this information. I record all non-alcoholic beverages that I consume.

- **Smart Scale:** I have a WiFi-connected scale that I use every day to weigh myself and to automatically record those measurements in a few connected apps. I like the scales that provide a variety of measurements beyond just weight such as BMI, body fat percentage, water percentage and such. Choose carefully because some smart scales just estimate those other metrics instead of measuring them.

- **Personal Fitness Tracker:** I use a wearable fitness tracker that continually measures my activity, heart rate and sleep to provide a constant stream of data regarding my fitness. I wear this tracker twenty-four hours per day except when I am in the shower. I am able to collect all of the data from the day and get a good picture of my overall health with this tracker. This is also how I get an accurate reading of the calories that I burn from exercise as it monitors my activity and heart rate during that activity.

- **Health App:** Finally, I use an app built into my phone that consolidates all of my fitness information from all of the other apps into a single combined view of exercise, nutrition, body measurements, sleep and other categories.

All of these gadgets and apps work together to help automate the tracking of my KPIs in order to measure my progress versus my plan. I can monitor both my important and my interesting KPIs and then some. I have also been able to learn a lot about my body and my habits using these tools and have used that information to improve myself.

Make it a Habit

When I was talking about the execution phase of your fitness project, I discussed how important it is to make your daily execution into a habit. Once it becomes a habit, you don't forget to do it and you rely on routine to ensure you are successful. This best practice also applies to your performance monitoring activities.

If you establish a daily habit for when and how you track your KPIs, you will be able to get consistent, apples-to-apples measurements and won't forget to do so. This is particularly important with your weight because you need to make sure that you weigh yourself at the same time of day wearing similar amounts of clothes (naked is better) and preferably before you consume any food or liquid. If you don't, you will get inconsistent results and less precision.

My daily habit starts the minute that I get out of bed every morning. I get up and go to the bathroom first thing. Once I am done in the bathroom, I step on the scale without any clothes on to get my daily weight rating without extra weight from clothes, food or drink. By doing this, I know that I am seeing just the weight of me and nothing else. I will weigh myself multiple times to ensure that I am getting a consistent weight two or more times. After I have my weight, I open the app associated with my smart scale and delete out all of the weight entries for the morning except for the one that I want to count as my "real" weight for the day.

Next I open the app for my wearable fitness tracker and let it sync with the tracker and with my scale. This captures the data from when I was sleeping and my resting heart rate in addition to downloading the weight from my scale. Once I have all of the data updated in my fitness tracker app, I sync it with my health app. The goal is to capture all of the data from various sources into this one app. As a final step, I also record my weight in my food tracker app so it can calculate my daily calorie budget.

My full morning data tracking routine takes less than ten minutes. Then I review the data to see if I need to pay particular attention to anything that day. For example, if I missed my exercise goals in the prior day, I want to make sure that I meet them for today. Then I eat some light foods to get my metabolism started, drink a glass of water and head to the gym.

You are going to be working hard in your project to manage your calories in and calories out to meet your goals. Throughout the process, you also need to remain vigilant about tracking your most relevant KPIs every day to ensure that you know how you are doing. If you properly leverage technology, this can be a quick process and you can spend the majority of your effort making progress versus tracking progress.

The biggest lesson I learned this week is that the numbers are just part of the story. My journey has lots of ways to evaluate success. For example this week I saw a distinct uptick in the amount of random people giving me positive feedback. It felt great!

OPERATION MELT
WEEK 19

Progress Reporting: Talk About Your Success, Even With Yourself

In any project, part of monitoring progress and KPIs is the preparation of routine status reports to share with project stakeholders. Depending on what you have chosen as your communication plan for your fitness project, you will want to produce periodic status reports to update on your progress.

At the very least, if you aren't talking openly about your project, you will want to share progress updates with yourself. I know this sounds strange, but it is part of how to keep yourself motivated. If you regularly remind yourself of the progress you have made versus your goal and your achievements, you will stay focused. Plus, if you compare your progress against the timeline you originally established, you may see that you are ahead of schedule (another great motivator) or that you are behind and will need some corrective action. Plus, you may be able to identify other problems that need to be addressed. Keep reminding yourself that you are making progress, you are doing great, you are killing it and that you aren't done!

If you have decided to openly talk about your project, you will want to provide some status updates to your stakeholders along the way. My suggestion is to do this once you achieve milestones versus sharing all of your updates along the way. When you share a status update with your network, make sure it is one that you are particularly proud of instead of just random information. If you do this, you will get tons of likes and comments about your update, and that will help motivate you.

In my *Operation Melt* project, I decided that part of my communication plan was to publicly share my journey. I did this early through in-person conversations about what I was doing and why. These in-person conversations increased frequency as my results started to become visible. My social media shares were more targeted and not super-public about my progress at first. I would check or post pictures during long walks if they were interesting, but I waited to share much until I hit my first milestone. Then in July, when I was just over a month into my journey, I posted the following:

Tony Weaver
July 20, 2017 · 🔒 ▼

So, I try really hard not to be one of those crazies that posts every single success or setback with their health and fitness. But, I need to take a second and share a proud accomplishment.

Through hard work (and mostly just smart decisions) I have officially lost OVER 25 pounds in the past 5 weeks! Woohoo!

Here's to the next 25! Now bring on lake week!

I waited until I had a big update, losing twenty-five pounds, before I went overly public with my journey. People were so supportive, and I got about a hundred likes and comments that were all very energizing. Then, I shared again at fifty, seventy-five and a hundred pounds with some other posts mixed in about specific things including showing some before and after pictures.

As you move through your journey, tracking your progress is absolutely critical, but sharing updates is important too. You are doing something big and are being successful with it and have earned the right to pat yourself on the back a bit. If you aren't comfortable sharing with everybody, make sure to at least share with a few close friends. But whatever you do, make sure to brag about your accomplishments to yourself. You need to continue to remind yourself that you are doing something important and you are killing it.

Next week is Halloween, and that presents a challenge for me. I am a big fan of candy and chocolate in particular. But those are foods that may be a setback for me. I am hoping that I can resist the temptation of those through Halloween. Fingers crossed, anxiety high.

OPERATION MELT
WEEK 20

Managing Issues & Risks: Staying On Course

One of the most important responsibilities for a project manager is to proactively manage project risks and address project issues. Put simply, an issue is something that has gone wrong that could prevent your project from reaching its goals within the agreed upon parameters or constraints. A risk is something that *might* happen that would compromise your project's ability to achieve its goals. A risk is something that can be proactively managed so it doesn't become an issue, and it is the role of the project manager to identify, prioritize and manage these risks. It is also the project manager's job to identify, prioritize and manage issues that have occurred until they are resolved.

Managing issues and risks is an important part of your fitness project. There are many risks that you can identify at the beginning and throughout your project that could prevent you from being successful. You need to identify what these risks are and think ahead about how you are going to prevent them from becoming issues.

At the beginning of your project, when you are creating your scope statement and project plan, spend some time thinking about what risks exist. Look through your scope statement and think about what things could happen that would impair your ability to achieve each of these items. Think about your behaviors, your lifestyle and your environment and consider where the barriers are. Also, do some reading about other people's journeys and understand what things harmed them along the way, and consider if those things are likely to impact you.

Once you have identified all of the possible risks that may impact your project, the next step is to determine how impactful each risk is. Think about each risk in terms of probability (how likely is it that this thing will happen) and in terms of impact (how bad will it hurt me if this thing does happen). Then for the items with the higher probability and impact, (or "risk exposure") spend some time thinking about what you can do to proactively reduce the probability or impact, or to "mitigate" the risk. This sounds like a complicated process, but it is a bit easier than you would think, and it is critically important for every project manager. Plus, it isn't a one-and-done process, you need to continue to do it over and over again throughout your project.

When I started my *Operation Melt* project, I identified several risks that I thought could be pretty impactful to my goals. A few of the risks that I identified included:

- If I will need a gym in order to start exercising, the start of my exercising will be delayed and may not happen at all.

- I may not have the discipline to continue focusing on my project for more than a couple of weeks if my results are not immediate.

- My job is very demanding, and my schedule is unpredictable. This may prevent me from being able to stay committed to my project.

This final risk is one that I actively took steps to mitigate. My job has always been one of my top priorities. I have not been good about setting boundaries. If work needed to encroach onto any aspect of my life, I would let it do so. Saying no or setting a boundary is not something that I had ever been willing to do. To make the situation tougher, I was at a point in my job where the pressure and workload had increased, there were budget issues, and I had a very demanding boss. The probability that this risk would occur was very high, and the impact was also very high. I needed to take steps to prevent this from stopping me.

As you know from the chapter on "calories out," I had decided that my prime time for exercising was first thing in the morning. I was already getting up at around 5:30 each morning, so getting up earlier wasn't a viable option to create the time for exercise. My alternate approach was to start arriving as work later than my normal 7:00-7:30 arrival time each morning. I decided to come in around 8:30 each morning instead. In the extra hour of time I gave myself every morning, I added exercise to my routine. Plus, as part of the scope of my project, I needed to manage stress by reducing work hours. So my best choice to mitigate this risk was to set new boundaries for work and start arriving later and leaving by 6:00 or earlier every night instead of later and limit work at home. As I mentioned in the project planning chapter, I built this decision right into my project plan so the plan itself helped me mitigate the risk.

The mitigation of this risk also created a new risk related to the change of my working hours. It was possible that the reduced work hours would result in a decrease in my effectiveness at work which would impact my success. The best response that I had to this new risk was that I had to make a decision on what was most important to me, my job or my life. Ultimately, I chose my life and decided to accept the other risk. If I became less effective in my role despite all of my best efforts, I would accept the consequences. My health, my life and myself had to become my priority, and that was a key decision that I used to mitigate a variety of risks.

Your fitness project is going to be a long and difficult project (a bit easier if you follow my *Operation Melt* process) and it isn't going to be one hundred percent smooth sailing. Through your journey, things are going to go wrong and you are going to have to respond. Watching for the issues that come up, determining out how impactful the issue is, identifying the root causes and figuring out how you are going to solve the problem is something you may need to do continually through your project.

During my journey, I encountered may different issues. I hit weight plateaus where my weight wouldn't change no matter what I did. I encountered times where my weight went up with absolutely no rational explanation. I found that my blood pressure was too high and needed to be addressed. I had aches and pains that developed including a nagging knee pain. Each of these issues needed to be evaluated and addressed through my journey.

One example of the issues that I encountered a couple of times is injury. There were three distinct sports injuries that I got through my journey - shin splints twice, strained Achilles once. At first, all I knew is that I had pain that was more than just a little post-exercise soreness. When this happened, I needed to identify what the real issue was. I did this by searching for my symptoms on the Internet and talking with other people who had similar experiences. Then I treated the issues with standard pain relief treatments including medicine and ice. I put all exercise on hold for a few days, though I felt terrible about doing so. I spent time figuring out the root cause of the injury. For the Achilles, my running form was very wrong, and I was able to correct that myself. For the shin splints, it turned out to be an issue with my shoes, and I needed to see a professional to properly fit me with upgraded shoes.

Unfortunately, each of my injury issues were high priority "blocking" issues because they prevented me from moving forward with my plan. I had to stop exercising in order to let the affected area heal so I didn't further injure it. As you can imagine, I worked with quite the sense of urgency to address and eliminate the issue to get the project back on track. This is typically the best practice for how a project manager should react to issues.

I have learned that weight loss impacts the size of your fingers. My wedding ring has started falling off. This means that I am at my smallest point in at least the nearly 17 years we have been married.

OPERATION MELT
WEEK 21

Managing Changes: Sometimes Things Happen

In the previous chapter, I said that one of the most important responsibilities for a project manager is to manage the issues and risks during the project. There is another equally important project management responsibility and that is to manage change. Change *will* happen during your journey for a variety of reasons — progressive elaboration, external events and the nature of life.

Let's start with that last item first, the nature of life. Change is a big part of life every single day. I want to share a couple of famous quotes about the constant state of change and our need to be adaptable. First, the Greek philosopher Heraclitus said, "The only constant in life is change." Meaning that we can depend on change happening and little else. Charles Darwin talked about how our adaptability to change is the thing that helps us survive when he said, "It is not the strongest of the species that survives, nor the most intelligent that survives. It is the one that is most adaptable to change." Put simply, change is going to happen and being able to react and adapt to it is your gift for being the strongest species. So bring on the change!

Why does so much change happen during a project? It is because of a concept known as "progressive elaboration" that affects all projects. The easiest way to explain progressive elaboration is that you don't know everything, but you are going to learn more as the project unfolds. When you start a project and create your scope statement and your project plan, you are doing it with the best knowledge that is available to you at the time. But, because your project is creating a unique product, service or result, that knowledge is a little bit limited. As the work of the project progresses, the project manager and the team will learn more. This new knowledge will often necessitate changes to the project. These changes can include adding or altering scope, changing the schedule, updates to the cost or other changes to the work, structure or project details.

Your fitness project is a place where progressive elaboration will certainly have an impact on you. When you start your fitness project you build a scope statement and plan that you think will get you to your goal. You include some very practical decisions in your plan and you adopt many proven best practices and then you start executing. But, until you are into execution, you don't really know if your plan is going to work. Once you learn more about your body and the world of health and fitness, you may have to update your plans.

As I explained earlier, when I started my *Operation Melt* project I decided that I was going to lose over one hundred pounds in under a year. I based this timeline on all of the best practices information regarding comfortable weight loss rates of two pounds per week. I assumed that the one-year mark was the right timeline. However, I reached one hundred pounds lost by the nine months point. So, my initial plan was no longer accurate, and I needed to change something. I either needed to change my timeline and say that I am "done" at nine months, or I needed to change my scope and take on more work and keep my twelve-month timeline. I could also do nothing, but that is not project management. You can't just let your project run on autopilot. As you will read in the final chapter of this book, I have adjusted the scope a little bit, but also celebrated success when I achieved my goal.

The final cause of change in projects is related to external factors that are likely out of your control. Imagine that you are leading a big project for a company, and they are suddenly acquired by another company. You didn't know that was going to happen, you didn't have any control over the decision, but it will certainly have an impact on your project, and you will need to react accordingly. As a project manager, the vast majority of changes that will impact your project are in this category because your project exists within a much larger environment that is always changing. It is the nature of life!

Your fitness project is certainly susceptible to externally driven change forces. While you have made health and fitness a priority, it is not the exclusive factor in your life. You have families, jobs, interests, friends and other responsibilities all competing for your attention, and you need to maintain balance. Sometimes this balance will require you to adjust your project plan for your fitness project.

During my *Operation Melt* project, I encountered many external factors that impacted my plans both positively and negatively. I already talked about the impact of injuries which sidelined me and ultimately stopped all weight loss progress for several days at a time. I also talked about how the weather turning cold caused me to lose my go-to form of exercise which was walking and running outdoors. When that happened, I had to add cost to my project by joining a gym which changed my plan. I absolutely should have expected that when I planned, but I didn't. This became a necessary adaptation.

The best example of an external factor that impacted my project was something that happened at the end of January. At this time, I had lost approximately eighty-eight pounds. One morning, I went to the gym, as was my routine, and then, after my workout, I got dressed and went to work. I got there right at 8:30 and went straight into a standing project meeting. Part way through the meeting, several people started getting pulled out of the meeting by their supervisors. My boss came to the conference room and pulled me out to go with him to a meeting. It was at the minute that I knew that there were changes coming. We walked into the conference room used by Human Resources where I learned that we were eliminating multiple positions that day, and I would be leaving the company where I had worked for ten years. Just like that, my job was gone, and I was starting a period of living on severance pay and beginning a job search.

This external change, that was out of my control, is one that had a few impacts to my fitness project. First, there was a positive impact because I had more time to focus on working out and moving the project forward. I could go to the gym for longer periods and go at different times during the day. That accelerated my rate of weight loss a bit and helped me get to my goal before the nine-month point. But this change also meant that my routine that I had established would no longer work for me, and I had to adjust my routine. This helped amplify my day-to-day weight fluctuations a bit because my routine was no longer, well, my routine. Plus, being out of work meant that I wouldn't be walking back and forth between buildings to attend meetings all day, so my general activity level would be impacted, and I would need to find a way to keep meeting my exercise goals. Finally, it meant that I had a second project that I was going to be launching to find a new job before my severance ended, and that project would be competing for my time.

Overall, the external change of losing my job could have had a significantly negative impact on my fitness goals. But because I was actively managing my project and actively managing my response to change, I was able to leverage this change for a positive impact on my project. Plus, having some extra time to focus on personal projects gave me the opportunity to write this book. I think that is a big win, but you will have to be the judge of that!

In the best practices of project management, a change-control process is used. It starts with identifying and defining the change, and what impact it will have to the project. The project manager (with other stakeholders) will identify the proposed response to the change including any scope, schedule, budget and other implications. This is documented in a change-request form of some manner and presented to the project sponsors for approval or rejection.

Good news! In your fitness project, there are no forms to fill out when changes happen. But you will still need to go through a very similar process. Start by realizing that something has changed. Maybe you have learned more, or maybe some external factor has impacted you. When this happens, pause and consider how this change is going to impact your ability to reach your goals that you have outlined in your planning artifacts. Once you have assessed the impact of the change on your project, it is time to figure out what you are going to do about it. Are you going to adjust your timeline? Are you going to change your approach? Are you going to take on new goals in the form of new scope items? How are you going to react?

Once you have made your decision, I would suggest writing it down the same way you handled the initial planning artifacts at the start of your project. Adjust all of your KPI targets accordingly and start tracking progress against the modified plan — or updated "baseline" in project management lingo.

Always remember that change is going to happen in your fitness project and that change is usually for the best. When the changes happen, you can let them sidetrack your project and make you fail, or you can leverage them and be better than before. The key is to review and react to changes in a calm and structured manner, and you will be a success.

I am realizing that this journey is a mental struggle too. My daily calorie target has dropped fast, but my brain doesn't want fewer calories yet. So I have cravings that I need to manage. I think the next chapter is going to be even more difficult.

OPERATION MELT
WEEK 22

Closure Phase: You Did It!

By mid-March, I was just two days shy of the nine-month anniversary of starting my fitness journey. The prior day, I had weighed at ninety-seven pounds down and was making good progress. I expected that I would reach my goal in another week or so. My apps were all projecting that I would get to the finish line within the next five to ten days. I was feeling pretty good and was excited to finally get to the finish line. Plus, I was going to get there early.

I woke up on this Tuesday morning and started my normal morning routine. I used the bathroom, brushed my teeth and stepped on my scale. I was expecting to see myself down ninety-eight pounds, maybe ninety-eight and a half pounds and was pretty pumped to be that far into my journey. What happened next was a huge shock to me... I saw the following on my scale. (Apologies for the poor image quality.)

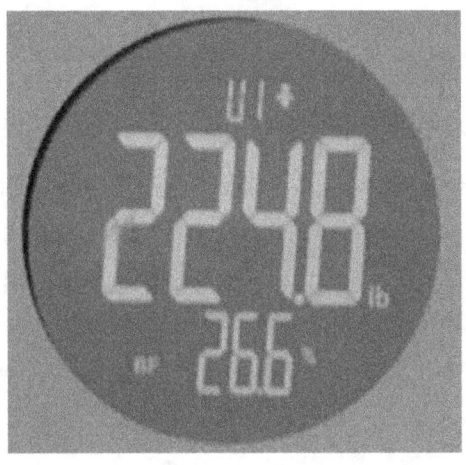

I had officially lost more than one hundred pounds in just under nine months in my fitness project. I was at the finish line and achieved my goal. In fact, I crushed my goal! This means that my project was done... kind of.

When you reach the goal that you set out in your charter and scope statement, you have officially reached the conclusion your project. This doesn't mean that you have to stop, but that your original project has delivered the results that you committed to deliver. So it is time to execute the closure phase for your project.

One of the first steps in the closure phase of any project is a fun one. The project team needs to pause and have a celebration. Your fitness project is no exception. When you hit your goal, you need to celebrate because you have just accomplished something big! You made a decision to get yourself more fit, you set an aggressive goal, you laid out a plan and you did whatever it took to get there. This is not a small feat and you deserve some fanfare. In fact, you should give yourself a couple of days to reflect on your accomplishment, and let it sink in a bit.

Once you have spent some time celebrating your achievement, you can work through the rest of the steps in the closure phase. The next two chapters discuss the two major steps to closing your fitness project.

This past week was Thanksgiving, and I definitely had some anxiety. This holiday tends to revolve around overeating. But I actually lost weight on Thanksgiving. I was able to have enough of everything to enjoy it, without it becoming a calorie bomb.

OPERATION MELT
WEEK 23

Transition To Maintenance Mode: Keeping The Weight Off

Once you are done with all of the hard work to achieve your goal, you don't ever want to slip backwards and have to do it again. So you need to figure out how to live as the new, healthier, fitter and thinner you. In project management, this process is known by many names and may be called the transition to "maintenance mode," to "operations," to "business as usual," to "keep the lights on (KTLO)" or something similar. Whatever the term, the idea is the same - you are done with the work of the project and need to continue to maintain the product.

The process for maintaining your weight is a little different from the process you used to lose the weight. The main difference stems from the definition of a "project" that we discussed earlier in this book. Let's pause to revisit that definition for a second:

A project is a temporary endeavor undertaken to create a unique product, service or result.

There are a few ways that maintenance mode differs from this definition of a project and they are pretty important differences. First, you are not creating a *unique product, service or result* because you have already done that. Instead, your goal is to continue to maintain the result that you have already created.

The lack of a defined SMART goal that you are working towards can sometimes be a problem for highly goal-oriented people. Because there isn't something that they are specifically working towards, they can lose focus. Sometimes people think of maintenance mode as no longer being fun, not exciting and no longer interesting. When this happens, people may end up slipping backwards in their fitness journey. There are many, many stories of people who have lost a significant amount of weight only to put it all back on. Don't let that happen to you!

You didn't come this far to only come this far!

The second major difference between maintenance mode and a project is an even more impactful one. The first part of the definition of a project is that it is a *temporary endeavor*. That is no longer the case when you enter into maintenance mode. This is not temporary. This lasts for the rest of your life, and you can't stop!

During your fitness project, you changed your lifestyle and habits in order to accomplish your fitness goals. You reduced the calories that you consumed every day and focused more on consuming healthy, wholesome foods. That is a change that you should permanently make to your diet. This is what helps you maintain the weight loss and healthiness that you achieved during your project. This is also why you should not aim to give up things that you love because that won't be sustainable for the long haul.

When you enter maintenance mode, you won't need as big of a daily calorie deficit and will be able to consume more if you so choose. When I first hit my goal, my tracking app told me that I could add a thousand more daily calories to my diet to maintain my goal weight. So you can adjust a little bit, but I would suggest not over-adjusting your calories, especially at first. Instead, get yourself into a solid diet routine that you are happy with and can sustain.

One of the first decisions you will need to make regarding your calorie intake during maintenance mode is whether or not you are going to continue tracking. If you have leveraged the process set forth in this book, you were diligently tracking everything you consumed in order to have a clear picture of your daily calorie consumption. Now that you are done with your project, you have a choice as to whether or not you want to continue doing this. If you decide to stop tracking your food, you cannot stop being mindful about what you are consuming. It is all too easy to fall back into the pattern of mindlessly consuming beyond your daily calorie target.

The other thing you were doing during your fitness project, was changing your habits to ramp up the amount of exercise you get every day. You were burning calories like there was no tomorrow and seeing the results of your work. You were watching yourself get smaller from a weight perspective and larger from a muscle perspective. Once your fitness project stops, your need to continue being active every day does not stop. You need to keep moving and continue maintaining a healthy amount of exercise. If you don't continue exercising, you will risk all of the progress that you made during your project.

Continuing to exercise on a regular basis does not have to be difficult. One of the best things you can do to continue to get exercise in maintenance mode is to join an organized activity. Do you like to play basketball? Then find a group to play with weekly. Did you learn to love running during your fitness project? Join a running group and participate in organized runs. Work to make exercise a hobby rather than just a commitment that you have made to achieve a specific goal. Your body will thank you.

Finally, if you are worried about your ability to continue to be successful in maintenance mode, you have another option. Don't stop focusing on goals. You can kick off a "Phase Two" of your fitness project, set a new goal, and repeat the process. The goals don't always have to be specific target weights, they can be other things. Do you want to train for a marathon or a 5k? You can start a new project and make that your goal. That is the magic of project management, it can be applied to a variety of goals and still be successful.

I will talk more specifically about my "Phase Two" in the final chapter of this book. But, for now, let's move on to the final step in the project management process for your fitness project and talk about hindsighting.

An interesting thing happened this week... I was at the gym and looked at myself in profile in the mirror. I really saw a difference. It is difficult to see your own weight changes, because they are so gradual. But I looked in the mirror at the gym and somehow I saw a clear difference in myself.

OPERATION MELT
WEEK 24

Project Hindsight: What Did You Learn?

A project hindsight, or lessons learned, or retrospective, is a process executed at the end of the project to identify any lessons learned from the project. This process often includes a review of everything that happened and is a collaborative process that engages all of the key project stakeholders. The goal is to identify those things that should be done differently in future projects and the things that worked well that can be applied to future projects. The hope is that the lessons learned from one project can positively impact the process or results for future projects.

Different project managers approach the hindsight process differently, and there is not a single right way of executing the exercise. The process that I like to follow is:

- **Project Recap:** Create a brief recap of the project timeline, results, process and any other facts regarding how the project was executed. This recap gets sent ahead of time to all of the participants in the hindsight process with a series of questions to use as thought-starters in the upcoming meeting.

- **Retrospective Meeting:** Conduct a collaborative meeting with the stakeholders to reflect on the project and to analyze it based on a number of dimensions (leadership, process, timeline, etc.). The goal is to collect all of the ideas of what went well and what could be done better.

- **Lessons Learned:** The full list of all of the ideas from the project team then get prioritized into a series of the most important themes. I like to try to boil these down to no more than ten big themes.

- **Hindsight Report:** The project recap and the prioritized lessons learned get combined into one final project artifact, the hindsight report. This report is a final summary of the project that gets delivered to all of the project stakeholders and sponsors and gets archived for future use.

As I have said throughout this book, this is not a project management book, and I try not to get deep into the specifics of the project management processes. I dug a little deeper into this one because I think it is really important in your fitness project. You have invested a ton of time and energy into this project, and it is coming to an end. This is a good time to figure out what you have learned from the project. If you learn lessons from the project, it continues to pay dividends well past you meeting your goal. Plus, many of the lessons you learn will likely include learning about yourself, and that is always a good way to help yourself improve!

Once you figure out what you have learned from your project, there is one important thing I would recommend doing with those lessons. Share them with other people! Throughout my fitness journey, I have relied on input from other people and the lessons they have learned in their own fitness journeys. I have read countless websites and social media posts from people that have executed a fitness project, and I was able to apply those lessons to make my own project better. I respectfully request that you share your lessons with as many people as you can. Maybe doing so will help contribute to the reduction of the obesity epidemic in America!

In the next section of this book, I will share my project hindsight report with you from *Operation Melt*. The project was very successful, and I learned a ton along the way. That is what inspired me to write this book.

Needless to say the first 6 months of this journey are shaping up to be very rewarding! I am looking forward to where I will be at the end of the next 6 months. I am confident that I will have crushed my goal of losing more than 100 pounds in less than a year!

OPERATION MELT
WEEK 25

Part 3: Operation Melt Hindsight Report

What Is A Hindsight Report

As I mentioned previously, a hindsight report is the final project management artifact delivered at the conclusion of a project. The goal of this artifact is to provide a recap and summary of what happened in the project as well as any lessons learned along the way. The delivery of this report marks the final closure of the project and signifies that the team and project manager are moving onto their next projects. It means the project is really, really, really done now.

For your fitness project, your hindsight report should similarly include a recap of the project. What happened and what were the results along the way? Plus, this is where you will capture your top ten lessons learned along the way. By reflecting on the project and the lessons learned, you will have the opportunity to remind yourself of how you did and how big of an accomplishment you had. Further, by documenting this information, you have a convenient resource to share with other people who are starting their own journey. Please do not underestimate the value of sharing what you have learned with other people. This is how we all help each other get better.

I ran my first mile without walking on Monday! It kind of happened by accident, and I built up to it, but it was a big deal for me. Hitting the one-mile mark is a first step for me and hopefully the gateway to a 5k where I can meet up with others and enjoy a run as a group.

OPERATION MELT
WEEK 26

Project Recap: My Results

I will begin my project hindsight report with my project recap. This recap includes a few pieces of information to present my results. I will start with the weight I lost, the other changes in my body size and some of the other things that happened along the way. Fortunately, I kept fairly diligent notes through my daily journaling and through my *OperationMelt.com* blog that I launched partway through my journey.

Weight Loss Results

As I shared earlier in the project plan chapter, I set out to lose over one hundred pounds in less than a year making my target date for completion June fifteenth. Then, I defined a few target milestones that I wanted to achieve along the way in order to ensure I was on track for this goal. Overall, my plan was to lose weight at an average rate of two pounds per week.

The following graph depicts my weight loss goal by day as represented by the red line that starts on June fifteenth of the first year and hits the one hundred pound mark on June fifteenth one year later. The second line on the graph, the blue line, represents my actual weight loss by day. You will notice that the blue line is not a straight line, there are many ups and downs and the rate of weight loss changes through the journey. However, I did reach (and exceed) the one hundred pounds lost point by March, three months ahead of schedule.

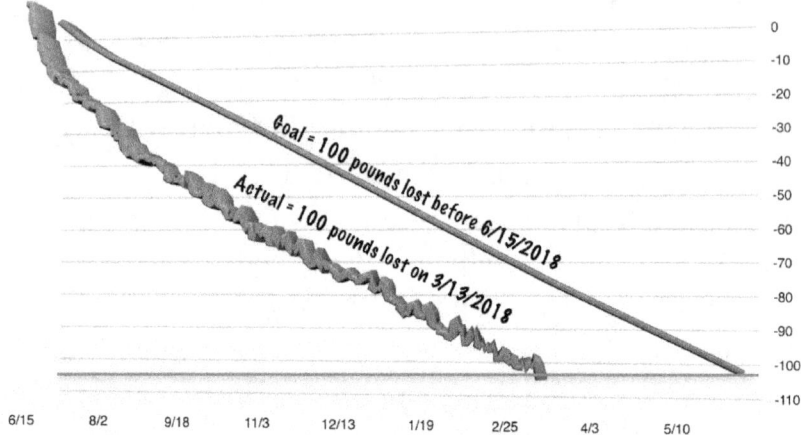

My weight loss was faster and more consistent earlier in my journey but was not as predictable as time went on. This is because my smaller body was more susceptible to daily weight fluctuations, and each pound represented a larger portion of my bodyweight and was a bit slower to burn off.

Other Body Changes

The scale was not the only place where I experienced changes in the shape and size of my body. I also changed clothing sizes multiple times through my project. This was most evident in the waist size on my pants which decreased significantly through the nine months of my *Operation Melt* project.

- June – the first month: When I started my waist size was about fifty-two inches though most of my pants were a very snug fifty-inch waist.

- August: I tried shopping for new clothes and found that, while I was definitely getting smaller and the clothes were starting to get really big on me, I had not changed in size enough that I could fit in smaller pants. I got frustrated and decided to give up on shopping for a while.

- September: I hit the fifty pounds lost mark and I bought new clothes for the first time in this journey. I really should have bought them sooner because my clothes had become comically oversized, but I wanted to wait until I hit the big milestone. At this stage, my waist size had shrunk to forty-six inches. I was only three months into the journey. I was down fifty pounds and down six inches. That was great! Plus, this was my last time shopping at big and tall stores. I was getting into normal sizes.

- November: I was starting to no longer fit in the pants that I bought just a few months before, so I bought another round of new pants. They were only two inches smaller in the waist, but they fit much better. This marked the point where I stopped getting the "relaxed" fit or baggy jeans. I was ok if the fit was a big more snug.

- January: Liz and I went shopping at a discount clothing store and I bought size forty-two jeans for the first time since high school. I was a full ten inches smaller than when I first started my journey!

- February: I bought size forty slim fit jeans and they fit perfectly! I could probably even have gone down to size thirty-eight!

- March: I reached the one hundred pound loss mark and all of my jeans are too baggy on me, and I am going to need to do some shopping again.

In addition to just seeing myself get smaller and smaller and needing to buy new clothes to keep up, I experienced lots of other changes in my body as well. Because I was doing tons of walking and ultimately running, the muscle tone and definition in my legs and butt got really great and nearly all fat in my legs disappeared. Plus, when I started weight training, I was focused on abs, chest and arms, and I really started seeing growth in my biceps and overall tone in my arms.

As I started getting smaller, my face started changing. I lost the fat in my face and I went from a round, minimally defined face with double chins to a way more contoured thin face. There was even a moment where I was walking into the house after dark one night and caught my reflection in the door and didn't even recognize myself. Every person you interact with usually sees your face, so these will be some of the most stunning changes for people.

1/31/2018
Before &

There were some other changes in the appearance of my body that weren't what I would think of as positive, though they really are. When I was three-hundred and twenty-five pounds, my skin was stretched to the point where it could completely cover that size of a body. Fast forward nine months later and I was a two-hundred- and twenty-five-pound body. Unfortunately, my skin didn't change at the same rate as the structure underneath it. So I had places on my body with very loose skin. The clearest example was under my arms where skin hung noticeably. It did not really look *that* bad, but it bothered me. I noticed it way more than other people. That said, I became proud of my gross skin because it was just a reminder of my journey. Some of this skin would ultimately tighten up as muscle developed, but some would not tighten up on its own. Fixing this would will surgery if I am that self-conscious about it. Spoiler alert: I really believe that I am not that self-conscious that I am going to get cosmetic surgery.

Health Changes

All of the visible changes through my journey have been fun because I, and other people, can see them happening, and they are great signs of progress. There have been many other changes that are not as visible that are even more important and impactful to my life. These are the changes to my health and wellbeing that are solid results from my work.

I wear a personal fitness tracker twenty-four hours per day with the exception of when I am in the shower. Because I do this, I can get solid measurements of my sleep cycles, my resting heart rate and my overall cardio fitness as measured by my VO score (I measurement of how efficiently my body makes use of oxygen). One very important change that happened through my journey is that my average resting heart rate - how fast my heart beats when my body is still - has decreased significantly. The following graph depicts the change through my nine month journey.

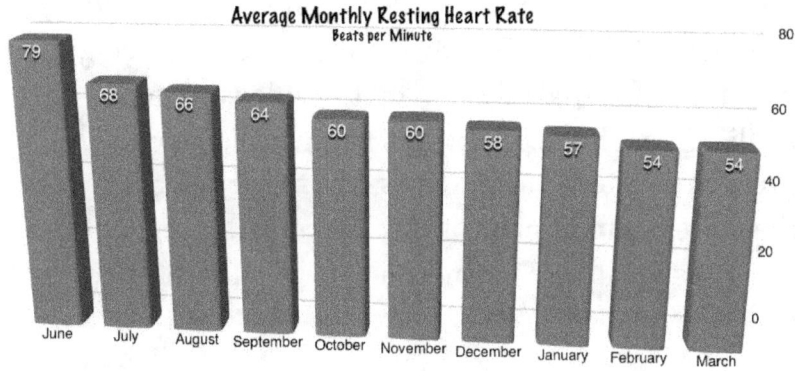

Average Monthly Resting Heart Rate
Beats per Minute

Why is it important that my resting heart rate decreased so much? Great question! First, as I said earlier, I am a numbers-driven guy, and this is another measurable thing, so it helped keep me motivated which is pretty important. This isn't the only reason that this number is important to me. The real reason is that the higher the resting heart rate, the harder that my heart has to work to keep me alive. I would rather make my heart's job a little easier.

Another important health improvement that I experienced during my journey is a lowering of my blood pressure. When I first went to my doctor in June, I learned that my blood pressure was pretty high. In fact, when I would check it at home through the week and then search the web for insight regarding the readings, I would see that I was very near the level that said, "Seek urgent medical attention." This is clearly not something you want to see. So my doctor prescribed blood pressure medication to help regulate my blood pressure. However, as I progressed further with my journey, I lost weight and improved my overall levels of activity. My blood pressure started getting better. It improved so much that I could stop the medication. This is great news because high blood pressure is often referred to as "the silent killer" because there are often no signs of high blood pressure, but the impact is great, and it can lead to organ damage and early death.

A final example of my improved health is the absence of something I used to have - aches and pains. When I started this journey, I had various pains in my body such as regular plantar fasciitis (pain in the bottoms of the feet particularly impactful first thing in the morning). I had knee pains and many others. As I have progressed through my journey, all of those random aches and pains have disappeared. Plus, I no longer have acid reflux, and I no longer snore. It is amazing how much being overweight and under-fit takes a toll on the body.

These are just a few examples of the areas of my health that have improved as I have gone through my fitness journey. There are many others that I discover regularly. In fact, nearly every measurement of my health has improved materially over the past nine months.

Fitness Changes

In addition to the positive impacts on my overall health and appearance, I have experienced many changes to my fitness. My physical abilities have increased as I have progressed through this journey, and I can do things now that I never thought possible just nine months ago. These abilities increase every day, and I am excited to continue to push myself to get better. I love setting new personal records!

When I started my journey, my exercise of choice was walking. I walked one or two miles before work each morning, and this paid great dividends in calorie burn. While walking was semi-low impact, it was still pretty draining for me, particularly on days where I would achieve over five total miles of walking. Just nine short months later, and I am running. I can run one mile without really even thinking about it, and I am starting to get that way with two miles. I have no desire to ever try running a marathon, but I want to be able to run a 5k whenever I want.

I have also seen improvements with my weight training abilities throughout the nine months of this journey. In fact, I really didn't start weightlifting until I joined a gym in October, so my gains in this space have really been over five months. I have continually increased the amount of weight that I can lift with bicep curls and ab crunches and have approximately doubled my maximum weight in both categories.

Throughout this journey, I have seen results nearly every day in some form. Whether it is being able to have killer workouts, seeing my weight drop, seeing my clothes pretty much just fall off of me or seeing my fears of dying early disappear, I have made progress. I am pretty excited not only about what I have accomplished so far but for the things to come. My journey doesn't end after this first phase of *Operation Melt*. It is just getting started!

Somebody told me this week, "You shouldn't worry about how much you eat between Thanksgiving and Christmas. You should just worry about your habits between Christmas and Thanksgiving." I completely disagree with this. Health and fitness matter every day!

OPERATION MELT
WEEK 27

Lessons Learned

As you may be able to tell by reading this book, I have learned a lot about myself, about health, about fitness and many other things through my *Operation Melt* journey. I have become very passionate about health and fitness for myself and others. I read about health and fitness every day, and I talk to as many people as I can about my journey and theirs. I have not learned this much in such a short time for a very long time and that makes me very happy. I am far from an expert, but I do have lots of knowledge, and I have a point of view.

Throughout my journey, I have been unbelievably appreciative for people who have shared the lessons that they have learned through their journeys. These lessons have been a big help for me when I didn't know what to do. Many of my challenges and questions were the same as other people, and they had already solved many of the issues. By sharing their lessons learned, I think they actually helped ensure my success.

This brings me to the final portion of my hindsight report: my lessons learned. As I discussed earlier, the goal of the hindsight or lessons-learned process is to identify those things that should be done differently in future projects and the things that worked well that can be applied to future projects. The hope is that the lessons learned from one project can positively impact the process or results for future projects. I can tell you firsthand, that the theory that lessons learned in one project help another is one that benefitted my *Operation Melt* project, and I couldn't have done it without these lessons.

With that as a backdrop, I want to share the top ten lessons that I learned through my project. I sincerely hope that these lessons can help you with your project. If nothing else, they will help you anticipate some of what you may experience as you progress through your journey.

Today is the last day of the year! Though there were several areas of my life where I was significantly less successful, my victories in my fitness journey overshadow those other areas. This resulted a great year for me! Happy New Year!

OPERATION MELT
WEEK 28

Lesson 1: This Is A Journey, It Is Going To Take Time

Throughout this book, I have referred to my *Operation Melt* project in a number of different ways. One thing that you may have noticed is that I frequently call this a "journey." This is because one of the biggest lessons I learned during this project was that health and fitness is not a destination. It is not someplace you get to and stop.

A lifelong commitment to health and fitness is made up of a series of never-ending experiences. Even getting to my *Operation Melt* goal was not instantaneous and took a series of twists and turns. It took me a while to start seeing the results beyond just the numbers, and it was far after other people started noticing the changes.

You can think about your health and fitness journey like climbing a high mountain. You don't just say, "See that mountain? Let's go climb to the top this afternoon." It takes time. You have to prepare for starting your climb if you aren't an experienced mountain climber. You have to take partners and leverage people who know how to get there, like Sherpas. You have to set realistic goals between the base of the mountain and the summit because you can't go straight from the bottom to the top. You have to take it one step at a time or risk failing with a big plummet to your death. You have to push through setbacks and issues as they come. And, you might not get to the summit on your first try.

Your fitness journey is very similar to a mountain climb. You have to set a reasonable goal and commit to it. Then you have to do research and take partners to help you build a solid plan to achieve your goals. You have to take one step at a time and build up to your ultimate goal. You have to deal with setbacks and push through adversity. You have to focus every day on the end goal. And you still might fail!

So, be ready for a commitment and a journey. Be ready for a lifestyle change in order to reach your goal. Take it one step at a time and build to your summit. But remember, unlike a mountain, there is more to climb after you reach the initial summit, and your journey is never finished. That is fine, because once you reach that first summit, you will want to go further.

My journey is getting more difficult, but the results are so visible to me now that it is stunning and a little emotional. In just 7 months and with just a little hard work, I lost 80 pounds (25% of my body weight). Why in the world did I wait so long to do this?

OPERATION MELT
WEEK 29

Lesson 2: This Journey Is Both Physical And Mental

Making fat go away in order to lose weight can be a very physical process. If you eat 2,000 calories per day, you are consuming 14,000 calories per week. Then, if your Basal Metabolic Rate says that you burn 2,000 calories per day at rest, you are purely at a break-even point and aren't losing any weight. If you want to lose two pounds per week, and one pound of fat equals 3,500 calories, you are going to need to figure out how to burn 7,000 more calories through your week to get there. This means you need to get more physical activity and get moving.

Imagine that you figure out how to burn 7,000 more calories in a week, and you are able to maintain the 2,000 calorie diet. You get to the end of the week, you get ready to step on the scale, and you are expecting to see two pounds go away. It is an exciting moment, and you are eagerly awaiting the results of your hard work. You step on the scale, you look down and presto! You gained, not lost, two pounds!

What you do next makes all the difference in the world. Do you say, "Screw it. This isn't working," and quit right there? If so, you are never going to make progress with this project. Your other option is to work to understand what might be causing the gain. It could be something as simple as the time of the day and the clothes you are wearing on the scale. There could be good reasons for the gain. But it requires you to have the perseverance to stick with the journey and commit to moving forward, rather than giving up.

This brings me to the second lesson that I learned during this journey. It is a mental journey, as much or more, than it is a physical journey. You need to keep your mind in a good place in order to be able to stick with it and make the progress you want to make. There are times where the journey is hard, there are times where it is emotional, and there will be times where the last thing in the world you want to do is go workout. You have to stay focused. That is why I keep saying that you need to make this a priority, you need to commit, and you need to know why.

As I was progressing through my *Operation Melt* journey, I had several moments where I needed to keep my brain in check or risk failing. There were some times that things happened during the journey that made me want to cry, and there were a couple of times that I did. There were external factors that made me want to put my journey on hold and focus on other things for a while. There were times where I questioned whether I could do it. All of this happened, and it made the victory that much more special.

One example of a place when I had to get my brain out of my way happened in November, which was five months into my journey. At this point, I had lost forty-nine total pounds, and I was doing a pretty good job. Because I had lost forty-nine pounds, my daily calorie target had decreased to 2,100 calories. While this calorie budget was more than sufficient to maintain my energy level and satisfy my hunger, I started to struggle with it. I came to the conclusion that one pint of a craft beer represented more than ten percent of my daily calorie allowance. I started to think that there was no way that I could stick to such a low-calorie allowance.

I can confidently say that this struggle was all in my mind and was an example of my brain getting in my way. I have since concluded that the issue was that my body had changed from a 325-pound person's body to a 275-pound person's body, but I still had a 325-pound person's brain in my head. My mental craving for calories decreased far more slowly than my physical need for the calories.

At this point, I was at a crossroads and had a couple of options. One option was to let my brain get in the way and sidetrack me. That would have essentially meant letting my body grow back to the size that my brain thought it was. This was not something I was willing to accept. The other option was to change some habits and figure out how to make my brain satisfied with the number of calories that my body needed. This is the choice I made, and I quickly got back on track. I am happily living within and under a calorie budget of 1,900 today.

A second time where the journey got mental and got a little emotional was in January right when I had reached the eighty pounds lost mark. I was writing an entry for my *Operation Melt* blog that I update every week. I was reflecting on my progress to-date and wrote the following:

> *My weight has been a negative part of my life for as long as I can remember. In just under seven months and with just a little hard work, I lost eighty pounds. That is about twenty-five percent of my body weight. Why in the world did I wait until I was forty to do this? Why did I let this problem persist for so long and be so embarrassing? I think I look like a different person, and I am not ashamed of how I look anymore.*

As I was writing this passage, I started to tear up a little bit. In fact, reading this passage again, two months and twenty pounds later, I still tear up a little bit. This journey is life changing and emotional, because I am dealing with something that has bothered me for my whole life. In just nine months, I fixed (at least partially) something that was an issue for forty years. It is something I had convinced myself couldn't be fixed. It is something that ultimately likely killed my father and would have killed me, so why did it take so long to take action?

Our minds are complex and messy things. We are very distracted, and we are spread very thin with all of the other things in our lives. We often need to be very deliberate about how we manage our brains and need to take steps to stay focused on our goals. In many cases, you are trying to undo things that have become habits for years, and that doesn't happen overnight. We need to give ourselves some space and time for our brains to grow. I am convinced that a fitness journey requires the brain to go through its own strength training in order to be what we want them to be.

I have embraced some tricks, exercises and routines to help keep my brain focused on the things I need it to focus on. Here are some examples in case you want to leverage them:

- Find your angle. I have said over and over that I am a numbers-driven guy and like to be able to track progress every minute of every day. I know that about myself and know that this is how to motivate myself. So, when I built my plan, I relied heavily on a numbers-driven approach. That is my angle. If you can find your own angle, you set yourself up for success from the start.

- Work in prime time. Each of us has times of the day when our brains are naturally at their best, and we can get our best work done. For me, this time is first thing in the morning before I get showered and start thinking about work. This is also when willpower tends to be at its highest. Use this time for your fitness project since this is now your priority. This is when I first added exercise to my routine. It is also where I added journaling. This was the time of day that I was most likely to stick to my goals.

- Knowledge is power. In order to continue keeping my fitness journey at the top of my mind, I spend a lot of time reading and talking about health and fitness. I try to acquire as much knowledge on the subject as I possibly can in order to continue to hone my skills and to continue to live, eat and breathe fitness.

- Strength in numbers. I am a very socially motivated person, and I can be very influenced by social groups in a positive way. That is part of why I started sharing details and accomplishments regarding my fitness project with people on social media. This was a way to continue to find motivation through others, both positive (congratulatory comments and well-wishes) and negative (a failure would be highly visible). This doesn't work for everybody, but it is likely to work if your brain is wired anything like mine.

- Nonstop search for motivation. I actively look for sources of inspiration and motivation daily to keep me going. Whether I am looking at some form of affirmation online, inspirational quotes, cool inspirational videos, music, art or whatever else, I am always looking for things to get me going. In fact, I have found a couple of great go-to videos that I watch when I am on the treadmill that cause me to workout harder than I do without them. Again, find what works best for you and go with it.

- Pass it on, pay it forward. Finally, I look for ways to share what I have learned and what has worked well for me in order to help others. I vividly remember the first time somebody told me that I was an inspiration for them and that they have also started a fitness journey. This was such a confidence booster and motivator that I try to find ways to help other people every day. Helping other people is effectively a multiplier of the impact of the hard work you are doing.

As you are starting your journey, just be prepared that there are some challenging days ahead and that a fair amount of this challenge is inside your head. Find ways to continue to stay focused and motivated, and you will get past those challenges. Remember that it isn't just your body that needs some fitness and shaping, it is your brain too.

I am having MANY opportunities to talk about my journey. People often ask me, "What's your secret?" I don't know if they are happy or sad when they hear that it is simply a commitment to knowing what I am consuming, managing it in a healthy way and layering on exercise.

OPERATION MELT
WEEK 30

Lesson 3: There Are Going To Be Lots Of Setbacks

In the last two sections, I talked about the mental impacts of your fitness journey and how you need to stay motivated in order to persevere. This motivation is so important because you are going to encounter lots of setbacks along the way. Success is a long and winding road - not a straight line. The more you set your expectations about this from the beginning, the better positioned you will be when things happen.

Through my *Operation Melt* project, I hit lots of snags along the way that I needed to figure out how to get past. These setbacks happen on a regular basis and require swift action to get through them without losing focus. I want to share a couple of my setbacks as some examples.

When I first started my fitness journey, I started walking as my exercise of choice. I tried to make sure that I walked one or two miles each morning before work and as much as I could on the weekends. A couple of weeks into my journey was July Fourth weekend, and we were at Indian Lake at our vacation cottage enjoying the nice weather. I decided to take a very long and brisk walk of nearly three miles and then have the family over where I would grill out (which includes lots of walking) and we would take a walk to see the sunset.

The result of this sudden ramping up of the exercise combined with an equipment challenge (more later) caused me to develop a painful condition known as shin splints. This is when increased levels of activity cause strain and overworking of some of your tendons and muscles. It is very painful and takes a while to completely go away. Attempting to just push through the pain causes the pain to be worse and stick around for longer. The only real solution is to rest the area.

There I was, two weeks into my newly prioritized fitness journey and I had a sports injury that forced me to skip exercising. This was bad timing and very frustrating, but I just had to deal with it and get through it without giving up. This was just the first setback and was definitely not going to be the last one. In fact, I gave myself shin splints a second time about a month later, and I strained my Achilles a month after that. Each time, the only solution was to slow down and rest, which I did and then got back on track.

Throughout this book, I have referred to calories in minus calories out as the approach for creating a calorie deficit. The calorie deficit will produce your weight loss as your body turns to stored fat to make up for the deficit. This is the way weight loss happens, and it is very scientific and mathematical. That is... until it isn't. Sometimes your weight loss isn't as immediately logical and mathematical as you would expect. This is the second type of setback that you are highly likely to encounter in your journey — fluctuations and plateaus.

Our bodies are complicated machines with lots of things going on at the same time. Plus, our bodies have a tendency to become accustomed to our surroundings and behaviors, and may react slowly or negatively to change. The result may be that your weight changes in unpredictable ways or doesn't change at all when you are expecting it to do so. I have found that my weight is often completely unpredictable on a day to day basis. When you are carefully monitoring your weight because you are trying to hit a goal, this can be very frustrating.

If you weigh yourself every day in the exact same environment (before or after using the bathroom, clothes or naked, before or after consuming food or drink, etc.), you are going to notice that your weight may change every day, and it will not always be down. It is normal for your weight to fluctuate a few pounds each day based on whether or not you have processed all of the food that you have consumed and if your body is retaining water. I have even found that certain foods and drink cause my weight to temporarily fluctuate up for a day. For me, high sodium and drinking too much beer (but not other alcohol) tend to cause my weight to fluctuate upward for a day.

The other thing you may notice as it pertains to your weight changes is that your body may have a natural cadence of weight increases and decreases. Each week, my Monday and Tuesday weigh-ins are always my best ones with the lowest weight. As the week progresses and I approach the weekend, the odds of my weight being higher are pretty good. These are probably lifestyle-related issues for me as we tend to cook at home more on Sunday, Monday and Tuesday and tend to go out Wednesday through Saturday. This is also where we may consume more alcohol and the beginning of the week I may not drink any alcohol at all.

I call these day-to-day weight changes "fluctuations" instead of calling them weight gains for one simple reason. It is nearly biologically impossible to gain one or two pounds of fat in one day, and these weight changes are just a result of your cells retaining water. That water weight then registers as a weight increase on your scale. Be prepared; the smaller you get, the more likely that these fluctuations are going to impact you.

A weight loss plateau is a much different animal and can be the most frustrating of all setbacks in a weight loss journey. A plateau is when you are diligently managing your diet and making sure you are getting plenty of exercise, but your weight loss suddenly stops, and it won't budge at all.

There are a number of different explanations for why plateaus happen, and there isn't one clear cause. Sometimes your body just adjusts to the level of exercise, sometimes your body decides to burn muscle instead of fat, and then your body also burns fewer calories as you get smaller after losing weight. Even an increase in stress, like worrying about the slowdown in your weight loss, can cause your weight not to fall. Since everybody is different, the causes of your plateau can vary widely.

If you encounter a plateau, you just have to stick with it and maybe change up your routine a little bit, and you should see the progress. If it is a prolonged plateau, it may be time to conduct a new fitness audit to see if there is something you are doing that is unhealthy like high stress, low sleep or something else.

I encountered a plateau about halfway through my *Operation Melt* project, and it was pretty frustrating. I hadn't changed anything and still had the same amount of high stress. I was eating healthy and was working out. For me, I believe that the lack of change in my routine was the issue. So, after doing research, I altered my workout routine just slightly. First, I started eating a handful of almonds in the morning before going to the gym to ensure that I was helping my body get started burning calories. Plus, I increased the intensity and decreased the frequency of working out for a week. That was enough to get me back on track and start the weight loss again.

I have mentioned stress a few times through this chapter and through the book. Stress is a major enemy of getting healthy and fit. In addition to having some significant health consequences, stress can make you deviate from your plan. Sometimes, the outside stressors make exercise the last thing you want to do and cause you to stress eat. This is why you need to find a positive outlet for stress. For many people, exercise is a good way to eliminate or manage their stress. Going for a run and just getting into "the zone" lets you separate yourself from the stress of your life for a bit. Yoga and mindfulness exercises such as meditation are also good tools to help manage the stress in your life. Whatever your outlet, actively managing stress is a must in order to avoid big setbacks or even sidetracking in your journey.

Throughout my journey, I had lots of sources of stress that were complicating my progress. I had a pretty high stress job, and I had a tough boss for a while who didn't make it easier to manage my stress. It was a rough time at the company, and there were some budget challenges and other issues that are beyond the scope of this discussion. This ultimately culminated in my boss leaving the company partway through the journey. Then there were new stresses associated with the leadership change and more budget challenges. Finally, at the end of January, there was a round of lay-offs to address some of the budget concerns and a group of people left the company. Unfortunately, I found myself in that group of people and was suddenly without a job after being with the same company for ten years. I had two choices for how to react to these events that were out of my control. I could be depressed and let it throw me off of my game, or I could recommit to my goals. I did the latter, I refocused on my fitness goals and ramped up my workouts now free from daily job stress. I gained even more momentum and got to the finish line just over a month later.

These are just a few examples of the setbacks that you may encounter during your fitness journey. Many of the setbacks will be completely out of your control, but you will need to control how you respond. You can use the setback as an excuse to quit or slip on your goals, or you can use the setback as motivation to achieve your goal. The choice is yours but only one of them is going to get you to where you wanted to be.

When you encounter a setback, pause and reflect on what the setback is and how it is impacting you. Then, reflect back to your charter and your moment of decision to get started on this journey. Go back and read your business case about why this journey is important to you. Take a minute to look at your progress so far. Then put the setback aside and get moving again. Don't give those outside issues or people enough power over you that they are going to knock you off of your game.

Over the past couple of months, the changes in my appearance have become pretty obvious. This week one of my coworkers told me that she didn't recognize me at first. That was a pretty validating and motivating reaction!

OPERATION MELT
WEEK 31

Lesson 4: Equipment Matters

The next lesson I learned that I want to share is about the equipment that you use when you get started with your journey. I was very surprised when I learned how much your equipment really does matter. The equipment you use impacts your safety, your convenience and ultimately the success that you will encounter. I will talk about a few areas where this impacts you: clothes, shoes and gadgets.

First, when it comes to selecting the right clothing to wear when working out, there are a few considerations. First, you want something comfortable that does not restrict your movements when exercising. You want to make sure that it fits well, which will likely be an ongoing challenge, because clothes that are too big can get in your way and too small can decrease your comfort and give you an excuse to stop.

When you select clothing, make sure that you choose something that doesn't make you too self-conscious about your appearance. I want to say that you shouldn't care about what other people think, and you shouldn't change your behavior because of their judgement. I agree with all those things, but I also know it is probably not practical to completely disregard what others think of you.

It is just human nature, and we all care. Don't let it be a distraction to you. Choose something where you know you look good. If you like how you look, that should serve you well.

Finally, your clothing needs to be weather appropriate — this is something I learned a few times when mine was not. If you are walking outside on a hot summer day, shorts and a tee shirt or tank top will be perfect. If you ramp up the intensity of your summer workouts and start running, you may want to invest in something that controls moisture to wick away the sweat. Sooner or later, the weather is going to start turning colder and you may need to start dressing in layers. If you decide that you want to go out for a run when it is ten degrees outside, you are going to need to choose clothing that warms you. There are all sorts of athletic clothes made for different weather conditions, and they really do matter.

The next piece of equipment that is absolutely critical are your shoes. You will want to choose these carefully and maybe plan to invest a bit more money than normal in good shoes. Your shoes are the shock absorber between the full weight of your body and the ground. You are relying on these shoes to provide you both comfort and support, and that isn't something you want to leave to chance.

I started off by just using whatever athletic shoes that I had laying around. There were many because I worked for a shoe retailer at the time. As I started ramping up the intensity of my workouts, this became a problem. I was putting my three-hundred-pound body in motion and was wearing old fashioned athletic shoes, which were designed to look good and not necessarily to take a good beating. Ultimately this is what led to my first bout of shin splints, because I wasn't taking the decision about my footwear seriously. This was ironic because I was a leader at a footwear retailer.

To adequately address your footwear needs for your exercise routine, I would suggest turning to the professionals. Find your local running store. These exist in most larger cities and are a great resource. Ask them to do a gait analysis where they video you walking on a treadmill to understand how you walk and your natural posture as that makes a difference in your shoe selection. Then ask them to measure you to figure out what shoe size you need. It may be different from what you think. They should measure you sitting down and standing up so you know if you arches flatten and your size changes. All of these should be free services and take less than an hour. Then the salesperson will make recommendations about specific brands and styles of shoes that will match your needs, as well as insoles or arch supports. Your goal is comfort and safety, and this equipment really does matter.

As a final equipment consideration, you need to think about your gadgets. This includes your personal fitness trackers, your "smart" things, your apps and anything else you use to track your journey. You want to invest in reasonable quality pieces that all work well together, or else you will have data everywhere and spend more time managing the data than working on your journey. In many cases, this means the fewer individual gadgets you have, the better, but you may not find one that you like to do everything. Once you find apps that you do like, I recommend upgrading to the premium versions so you have all the features. You may need to use trial and error to figure out what is best for your journey.

This is an important journey and you need to make sure that it is one that you will stay with through the end. Make sure that you have the right equipment to help you.

Sometimes the daily ups and downs and other noise in life make me lose sight of the bigger picture in my journey. It is easy to encounter a minor setback and let it be discouraging. But, just when that happens, there are new wins that make me step back and say, "Wow!".

OPERATION MELT
WEEK 32

Lesson 5: You Aren't In This Alone - That's Good & Bad

Unless you live alone on the side of a mountain, you spend your days surrounded by people. Some are people you know, and they are your family, friends and colleagues. Others are people you kind of know like the waiters and bartenders and baristas at your favorite haunts. Then there are people you don't know at all who are just strangers on the streets — the extras in the film of your life.

No matter how hard you try, your personal fitness journey will not be private for long because people will notice. Then, there is one other thing that is completely certain, once people notice, they will speak up about it. It is amazing how much people are willing to walk up to you and make comments about your weight when they see it decreasing. It is probably good that people don't do this when they see it increasing. "Hey, I see you are putting on weight, keep up the good work!"

If you aren't prepared to have random strangers talking to you about your weight, you are going to be pretty surprised when it starts happening. In general, most of these things are fine and supportive statements to hear.

They should make you feel great about the progress you are seeing in your journey. You should count them as just one more milestone that you have hit. But, don't spend too much time analyzing the alternate meanings or the insulting things that they imply. It is best to assume that was unintentional. Here are some of the common statements I have heard along the way:

- "Have you lost a bunch of weight?" This one is an example of a person trying to confirm what they are seeing and to congratulate you. But it feels a little awkward when they quantify the weight with terms like "bunch" or "ton" because that means I used to be a "bunch" overweight.

- "You are just melting away" or "the incredible shrinking man" are ones that I get often. These are fine, they make me feel good, and they are the inspiration for the name of my website and my book!

- "Wow, I didn't even recognize you!" This one is a pretty validating and motivating reaction to get. I am not trying to become a different person, but I kind of am trying to become a different person.

- "You must feel so much better!" This is a reaction that I get at least once a week and it is a head-scratcher for me. I didn't feel bad before and wasn't aware of any ways I was struggling in my life. So it isn't that I feel "better" per se, but I do feel different. I have a bit more energy. I am way more aware and deliberate in my life. I am trying new things that I didn't know I was missing. However, when spending a day completely sore from a workout, I am not necessarily feeling "better" than I may have felt a year ago.

- "How much do you weigh?" This is a question that started coming late in my journey that I never thought people would be so comfortable asking me. People know that I am working on losing weight, and they have seen the progress, so they think I obviously want to tell them what I weigh now. The first time it happened, I was kind of taken aback by the question. Eventually I became more comfortable talking about it, and it wasn't as strange of a question...but really it is still a little strange.

These are just a few examples of the things that people will likely say to you about your fitness journey once they start seeing the results. Again, in general, they are fine statements meant to be supportive. The ones that are a bit more awkward are the ones that get said to other people about your weight loss.

- "Is Tony ok?" Is one of the earlier reactions that I got, and it was through somebody else. This colleague of a colleague noticed that it looked like I was losing weight and was concerned. This was an awesome moment for a couple of reasons. First, this may have been one of the earliest instances of a random person noticing my results, so that's fun. Plus, this person who hardly knows me expressed concern in my well-being. That kind of makes me happy for humanity in general.

- "Tony isn't even overweight anymore. He's just like a normal guy." When I heard this, it made me chuckle a bit. First, it is an uplifting statement because I was, in fact, still overweight and was working to lose sixteen pounds more on my journey. To have somebody say that I was not looking overweight was great, and it was the first time in my entire life that I have heard that. However, the implication was that when I was overweight, I was not a normal guy. I know this is not what the person meant, but this is really a statement of the impact that body size has on society's perceptions of you as a person. Deep, right?

- "You must be so proud!" This is one of two statements often said to my wife when people are talking about my weight loss. This is a very interesting sentiment, and I am not sure what it really means. Liz and I have been best friends for over twenty years, and my size and her size have never been a dimension of our relationship. Are people saying she is proud because I have set a goal and worked my ass off to try to meet that goal, so it is pride in my determination? Or is it pride that you finally have a smaller, right-sized man? I am not offended, and I don't think she is either, but I am really not sure what the intent is of this one.

- "You better watch out, Liz, if he keeps going!" This is the other comment that my wife hears a lot, and it is a bit more offensive (though I know that is not the intent). I am sure this is an innocent statement to humorously show support; unfortunately, there are several possible disturbing meanings of this. First, it could be interpreted as, "Wow! Tony is almost thin enough that people will finally find him attractive, and you are going to need to be jealous Liz." If that is the meaning, this compliment kind of sucks. If it means, "Tony is going to be attractive and choose a different mate," the compliment really sucks even more. Or, if you put those together, it could mean, "Tony is going to be attractive. Women are going to start throwing themselves at him, and he is going to cheat on you." This is the worst possible meaning. While the rock-star feeling sounds fun on the surface, my size has nothing to do with my integrity.

These statements are an example of how the people around you are going to try their hardest to be unbelievably supportive. A successful fitness journey in America is pretty rare, and people, mostly, want you to be successful. I say mostly because there are some people who may not be as supportive as you would like because they see your success as a threat to their way of life in some way. This is very rare, and fortunately people are more often supportive. If their show of support seems less supportive than you would hope, just remember that they tried.

Being prepared for when people say something to you really is one of my biggest recommendations through your journey. You may want to have your elevator speech ready, because people will approach you with some common questions. How might you respond when people say things like, "Congratulations, you look great!" This is an easy one, because you can just thank them, minimal speech needed. Many then will then go on to ask something like, "What is your secret?" They may assume that you are latching onto some fad diet or something that is helping you, and they want to do it too. The other common thing you will get asked is, "What made you do this?" People will want to know your story. So make sure that you have your answers ready so you are prepared to give answers you are comfortable with giving.

One way that people will want to engage with you is that they will want advice on how they can be successful with their own journey. Like it or not, you are going to become a fitness consultant once you demonstrate success. I actually liked this part of the journey and was happy to share my knowledge and experiences in hopes of helping other people.

Similar to the people asking you for advice and guidance regarding your fitness journey, you should be doing the same with others. Lots of people are way ahead of you on their own journey, and they are usually willing to talk about it. The more input and perspectives you get from others, the more likely you are going to be successful. I talk to lots of people about their routines and their lessons learned, and it is helpful for me.

One great example of how I leverage other people happened when I started running. I just jumped right in and really had no idea what I was doing. How hard can it be? It is like walking, just faster, right? Then I noticed that my endurance and distance weren't improving the way I thought they should, and I started talking to my friends who are runners. I asked about their normal running pace and how they selected that pace. I asked about how they have trained for races and events. I asked about what they do differently between treadmill and outdoor running. I even asked about their underwear! Every time you answer somebody's question, or they answer your question about fitness, we all get healthier and that should be our goal.

When I started this journey in June, I set a goal of losing over 100 pounds in under a year. I thought it was an aggressive goal, and I would likely not achieve it in that timeframe. I will hit 90 pounds by the end of January, so my 100-pound goal is really in sight now. Then what?

OPERATION MELT
WEEK 33

Lesson 6: There Are Going To Be Surprises

One theme that I have talked a little bit about up to this point was how I was surprised by a number of things during my journey. It seemed like every step along the way there was something that happened that was unexpected. In fact, a significant portion of these chapters about lessons learned are about surprises that I wanted to share with you, so you were not completely blindsided by them. In this chapter, I will share a few additional lessons that I learned through my *Operation Melt* journey that don't fit elsewhere in the book.

I was the last one to see myself changing.

When my journey first started, I was quickly able to see the changes on the scale and through other empirical measurements. But, I wasn't seeing changes in my appearance. People started coming up to me and complimenting me on my weight loss, and saying how different I looked. Some people were even specific about how they saw the differences in my face or how my clothes were fitting me. But, I still couldn't see the difference myself.

I have a theory that it is hard for us to see the physical changes in our own bodies for two reasons: over-exposure and prior conditioning. First, we all see ourselves each day for some period of time. I see myself naked in the mirror in my bathroom, and I see myself clothed in every reflection I walk by. I saw myself every single day, so the changes in my body may have been happening so gradually that I could not see them. Want to test this theory? Once you have lost twenty pounds, schedule a lunch with somebody who hasn't seen you since you started your journey. Their reaction will be much different from the one you will get from the person who just saw you last week. Gradual changes are always less impactful and harder to notice than significant ones.

The second reason that I believe it is hard to see the changes in our own body is how we have conditioned ourselves. When I was larger, I really did not like how I looked in the mirror, in pictures or anywhere else. I tried very hard not to look at myself. Through years (decades) of doing this, I stopped noticing myself, and my brain would effectively look past my physical appearance. This didn't stop when I started moving in an improved direction.

Though you may not see your own changes immediately, please don't get discouraged or give up. You will see the changes every day through the numbers that you are tracking through your day-to-day measurements (weight, heart rates, etc.). As I will talk about in another chapter, you will certainly see a difference in your clothing size as you rush to replace the clothes that no longer fit. Plus, you will hear about your changes from other people, and that will be a motivator. Just keep going, and you will eventually start seeing it yourself. When you really notice the changes in your appearance, it will stop you in your tracks!

I really started caring about how I looked.

Once I started really seeing the changes in my appearance, I quickly broke free from the conditioning that I just talked about. I started noticing myself all of the time, and I was paying attention to what I was seeing. I really started to care how I looked and wanted to put my best foot forward more than ever.

For several years now, I was a little interested in details and improving my daily care routines. Once I started caring more about how I looked, I really started upgrading my daily routines. For example, I switched from my standard, no-frills bar of soap in my shower to moisturizing soap. I tossed aside my old can of standard shaving foam and upgraded to a badger-hair shaving brush and cream set followed by an after-shave moisturizer for my face. I stopped going to the nine-dollar haircut place and moved to a Tonsorial Parlor for my haircuts including finishing with a straight razor - and cuts happened more frequently because I noticed when my hair was too long. I really started becoming attracted to smaller details in my routines and environment.

It wasn't just in my personal care routine where I started to be more sensitive to the details of my appearance. I started to become more aware of when clothes weren't fitting me properly and were baggy. This is when I moved to new and more snug cuts for my jeans. I even tried out slim fit shirts and clothing because I didn't like how the other cuts made me look bigger than I really was.

Finally, and this one is a little bit stranger, I really noticed when my muscles started to grow and become firm. I know it sounds odd, but I started often putting my hands on my butt when I was climbing the stairs because it was so firm when it flexed. I put my hands on the front of my thighs when walking down the stairs for the same reason. Then, my biceps started to grow, and I started flexing them often and talking to my wife about "the gun show." Then, I got concerned because I thought my left and right bicep weren't symmetrical. I got a little bit crazy and really paid more attention. Hey, I had lots of years of ignoring my body to make up for and started to do it all at the same time.

My body changed in strange ways.

The main purpose of my entire journey was to change my body to get thinner and healthier than where I started. With this goal, I expected to see changes like my stomach, chest, thighs and other areas of my body get thinner. This occurred as expected, but there were other changes that happened to my body that were more unexpected.

One change that I experienced around the time I had lost sixty pounds was that my fingers started getting smaller. This meant that my wedding ring started getting a little big on me. One day I was in a meeting at work and gestured with my hand and flung my ring across the room. I was fortunate to find it, but knew then that I needed to invest in a temporary ring adjuster. This was effectively a wrap that goes around the ring under my finger to make it smaller. I then planned that when I arrived at my final maintenance weight, I would ultimately need to get the ring professionally resized.

A second unexpected change happened to my feet. Once I hit the hundred pounds lost mark, I started seeing my shoes get a bit bigger on me. The length of my foot was still the same, but they were getting narrower. Because I was really not even sure what my real shoe size was, I opted to get professionally measured.

Once I had lost about sixty pounds, I learned that my skin did not shrink at the same rate as the body underneath it. In fact, based on research that I had done, it was likely that my skin would never fully shrink to fit my body. I had to come to terms with the reality that my skin would mostly remain as fitting a body that is over a hundred pounds larger than me. I saw it as particularly impactful on my neck, under my arms, on my thighs and on my stomach.

When you are in the midst of your journey, pay close attention to how your body changes, because it may be different than what you might expect. Plus, the shrinking of your body produces some other surprising side effects.

I got cold!

Through my journey I lost one hundred pounds of my body mass which translates to having over one hundred pounds less body fat. This was great and exactly what I hoped for. But, once the first winter rolled around, and I was down about eighty pounds, I discovered that body fat is a great insulation. I was very overweight my whole life and had this extra insulation keeping me warm. Suddenly it was gone, and I really felt it.

On one of the first cold days, my wife and I decided to walk through the park in our neighborhood to take some nighttime pictures of freshly fallen snow. The temperature outside was cold, but it wasn't excessively cold. It was probably only twenty degrees or so. But, I was so cold, even in my coat, that I was shivering and couldn't stay outside. It was terribly uncomfortable, and I thought I was going to die. The rest of the winter was full of abnormally low temperatures and not fun.

After losing so much weight, this was the first time that I had even been so cold. My wife tells me that she thinks it is the first time I have really been cold at all. This was a big, unpleasant surprise during the winter, but would be more pleasant during the summer. When the weather gets hot, I used to get very hot and feel miserable. My smaller body meant that I was not as hot in the summer, and I enjoyed warm days more.

My tastes, tolerances and sensitivities changed.

Like any person, there are foods and drinks with tastes that I really like and some that I don't care for, or I actually hate. As I progressed through my journey, I found that some of these tastes started to change. There were foods that I really started to like and crave that I previously hated; examples included avocados and hot tea. There were also things that I used to like that I no longer liked as much; sweets are a good example and are usually disappointing now. This was kind of a shock and led to me becoming a way more adventurous eater.

Additionally, as I started getting significantly smaller (having lost over fifty pounds), I began to notice a change to my alcohol tolerance. I could no longer consume as many alcoholic drinks before starting to feel buzzed or drunk. This is a change that I had sort of expected after a friend of mine experienced this after significant weight loss. But, it was surprising when it first started happening. The good news is that I don't drink as much and that helps control calories.

Beyond having different tastes and losing some of my tolerance for alcohol, I noticed other changes in how my body responds to what goes inside it. When I was over three hundred pounds, I could put anything in my stomach and not see any effects of it. That became no longer the case, and I needed to be more aware of certain things. Sodium, for example, is something I never paid too much attention to, but then it started to throw my weight into a tizzy because of water retention. My caffeine intake, which was previously unlimited, had to become way more controlled because it caused me to get wired and for my heart to race a bit - something that wasn't happening before. Plus, I had noticed some foods having more of an impact on my digestive system and changing the speed with which food gets processed through and out (too much information?).

I got judged for my focus.

As you probably know by now, I did not keep my journey a secret along the way. I posted frequently on social media. I talked to people about it often, and people started seeing the results. People were very supportive of what I was doing and very complimentary of me. For the vast majority of the journey, all of the feedback I got was great, and I was very happy.

Unfortunately, there were some outliers to the completely supportive and well-wishing comments that I received. There was at least one instance where somebody believed that my focus on my health meant that others weren't important to me any longer. This person, a coworker of mine, believed that I shifted my complete focus to my fitness, and that I no longer cared about the people who worked for me or with me. However, that wasn't the case at all, and there were other circumstances affecting this particular relationship. But, the person defaulted to blaming my fitness journey because it was an easy target. Then she judged me for lacking commitment or concern about my job, something that was false.

Your changes along your fitness journey will be very visible. Plus, if you go public with your journey, people will know that it is an important area of focus. Because of this, it will become an easy thing for people to blame when something doesn't go their way. It is unfortunately, but it happens, and you need to be ready for it.

I needed to eat more to lose weight.

I talked about this a little bit in the chapter about setbacks, but there were a couple of times along my journey when my weight loss plateaued. There I was minimizing my calories going in and maximizing my calories going out through lots of exercise. I was sweating every day, I wasn't overeating, and I suddenly stopped losing weight. WTF?!

It turns out that the secret to why I stopped losing weight was that I wasn't eating enough calories. My calorie burn had increased so much that I needed to fuel my body more. This simply made no sense to me! I had to eat more food, particularly meat (which I love,) in order to lose weight. How could that be?

All of the sources that I researched said that I was over-training. This included the component of failing to give my body enough calories to start its fat burning furnace. In essence, my body was going into starvation mode and trying to maintain fat reserves instead of burning fat. Thus, my weight just held steady.

Though it challenged my new-found habits, I took a couple of days where I slowed my exercise a bit and ramped up my carnivorous habits. I ingested about 120 grams of protein and consumed a fairly high amount of calories day. The next day - Boom! My weight started decreasing again, and I dropped four pounds in a single week. I learned that with more and more exercise, my calorie consumption continued increasing.

It turns out that in diet and exercise, like anywhere else in your life, there is a very real concept that too much of anything is not a good thing. Everything requires balance.

I got called a very shocking name!

One morning, I was at an appointment with my doctor, and he called me something that really shocked me that I will never forget. I was asking him about my daily protein intake. I had done lots of research and opinions varied widely regarding how much protein I should be trying to consume every day. So, I asked my doctor about it. He decided to look up the right amount based on my weight and activity level right there in front of me, and that is when he said, "Based on your level of exercise, you need to be looking at the protein targets for athletes."

Wait, what?! Did my doctor just call me an "*athlete*"? Just a few months ago, I was stepping on his scale and found out that I was 325 pounds. I had no idea of any of my vitals or other aspects of my health. I was in terrible shape and blissfully ignorant about it. Then, just eight months later, he was calling me an athlete. Wow!

> *Today was another milestone for my Operation Melt journey... I finally hit the 90 pounds lost mark (91 actually). This is the last incremental milestone before the big goal. I think I am only a month away, and I can't believe how close that is!*

OPERATION MELT
WEEK 34

Lesson 7: Clothes Are An Issue

Earlier I talked about buying new clothes and how it was a sign of my positive body-changing results. I spoke very positively about it and, in general, the need to buy new clothes is a great thing because you are making progress. But, I do want to say that it isn't a completely positive experience.

Having to continually choose between buying new clothes, or looking bad in oversized clothes, sucks! I waited a long time in my journey before going through my first round of buying new clothes. I can honestly say that I looked terrible by the time I pulled the trigger. I was wearing clothes that were meant for somebody fifty pounds heavier. I was relying on belts to keep the clothes on me and had several close calls with falling pants. It was bad.

The following is a picture of me wearing my original jeans after I had lost ninety pounds. You can see why I needed new clothes for sure!

So, I dropped a couple hundred dollars on three pairs of pants and three new shirts. They fit much better, and I was happy with my choices. Fast forward a few short months later, and I had to rely on those belts again to wear those pants. I could still wear the shirts, but they looked way too big. In that year, I had to replace an entire wardrobe three times (four for some items).

Here is a picture of three generations of jeans for me. Note the tape measure to give some sizing perspective. There is a six-inch difference on one side.

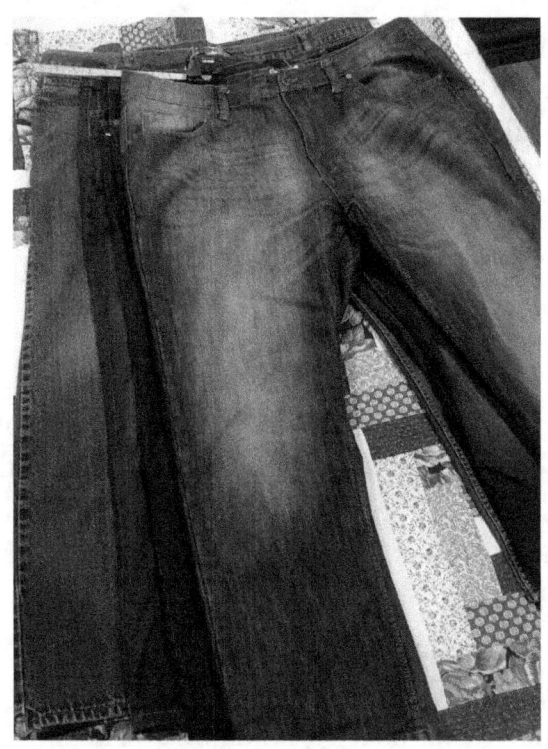

Then came the time when I knew that I was going to have to start interviewing for new jobs. I had to make the decision to buy a new suit. The only suit I owned was one that was a bit big on me when I was ninety pounds heavier. I knew I needed something but didn't want to invest a ton of money into a single outfit that was likely only going to fit for a couple of months. Fortunately, I found a Valentine's Day sale and was able to get an adequate suit for under two hundred dollars.

It was difficult to reconcile buying new clothes, knowing it was essentially throw-away spending, versus the bad feeling of wearing clothes that didn't fit and weren't flattering to my new body. One thing that helped was that I knew I had clothes in various sizes that no longer fit me, and that it is often very difficult for nonprofits to find large clothes that fit their clients. I knew I could donate these clothes to people who really needed the help.

Another positive side effect of getting smaller was that the options for where I could buy clothes exploded. Previously, I could pretty much only go to big-and-tall stores which got me what I needed but with very limited options. After all the fitness work, I could walk into pretty much any clothing store and find things that fit. Plus, I was able to purchase things that I would never have expected. I never even considered clothes such as slim-fit shirts and skinny jeans. It was as if a whole new world of options opened up to me, and it was thrilling to take advantage of this!

As I have been interviewing, I have learned that my journey has become a big part of who I am. The planning, focus, discipline and analytical approach I have brought to this journey speaks volumes about what I can bring to other aspects of my professional life.

OPERATION MELT
WEEK 35

Lesson 8: Yes, You Can Indulge... Mindfully

When I started my *Operation Melt* project, one of my goals was that I didn't want to give up any of the things I enjoyed. I enjoyed restaurants, happy hours with friends, beer, wine and bourbon. All of these things present challenges for somebody who is trying to manage their calorie intake. Excessive amounts of calories hide inside these things. All can be a calorie bomb waiting to happen.

The good news is that you can indulge on these things even when you are trying to manage your calorie intake. In fact, I would go one step further and say that you should indulge on things when you are trying to get healthy. By doing so, you will remind yourself that you can enjoy the journey, and it will be more likely that you can stick with it. You just need to be careful about how you approach indulgences such as restaurants and drinking.

Your Secret to Indulging: Mindfulness

The biggest enemy of your fitness journey is anything that you do in a mindless fashion. You have to be completely aware every time you put something in your body. For example, let's consider going out for happy hour with your friends or coworkers.

We will start with the drinking. Depending on your drink of choice, drinking just two craft beers per hour at a three-hour event could result in more than 2000 calories. But, the drinks are just part of the story. Often, the drinks are accompanied by snacks like nachos, wings and other junk food. A couple of buffalo wings plus sharing an order of loaded nachos could add up to another 500-800 calories or more. So, in just three hours, you can mindlessly consume more than your average daily calorie target. The excess calories are just the tip of the iceberg. There is also the fat, cholesterol, the slowing of your metabolism and other unhealthy gifts.

There is a better way for your fitness goals to survive the office happy hour. Just make sure to adopt a few common-sense strategies when you are indulging.

Strategy Number One: If You Want to Win, You Have to Keep Score!

As I have talked about through this book, data is your friend in a fitness journey. The biggest enemy of fitness is mindlessly putting things into your mouth. Happy hours and eating out make this trap even easier to fall into. You are talking with friends, people around you are mindlessly ordering, there are tons of choices, and your mind is elsewhere.

The trick is to pause, and think, and keep track. The easiest way to do this is to plan to log all of your food and drink selections in an app or other tracking tool. I recommend an app because it is possible to make choices based on nutrition facts. Just pausing to make a note of what you are consuming (or, even better, planning to order) is enough to put your brain in the moment and to help you make better choices.

When you are logging your food, pay particular attention to the things served on top of, or beside, your snack. Sauces, melted cheese, dips, dressings and so on are places where calories hide. You may choose to splurge on the six chicken wings at a hundred calories each, but the buffalo sauce may add another fifty calories. Then you have the ranch or blue cheese dressing and you are facing an over-the-top calorie bomb.

Strategy Number Two: Choose Wisely!

It sounds obvious enough, but different drinks have different calorie contents. For example, the well-known light beers total just over a hundred calories for a twelve-ounce bottle, whereas a craft beer triple IPA may be double or triple that (tip: higher ABV usually equals higher calories). A slow-sipping glass of red wine is about 125 calories which is just about the same as that gone-in-an-instant shot of cinnamon whiskey.

My approach is to start with one higher calorie drink and then move to lower calorie drinks. I always drink a full glass of water with each alcohol drink. Also, I will gravitate towards drinks that I know I will consume more slowly. I am a bourbon fan, so a bourbon neat will be something that I absolutely will not drink quickly and is only about a hundred calories. A rate of one-hundred calories per hour is very respectable for a happy hour versus having two 300 calorie IPAs during the same time.

Strategy Number Three: Size Matters!

Just because that light beer is lower calorie, doesn't mean you should order the thirty-two-ounce bucket of it as your drink. Like anything else, portion sizes of drinks can quickly get out of control and lead to over-consumption of calories. Don't let this happen to you!

Try to always default to the smallest size available for drinks. This may mean choosing the twelve-ounce beer versus the twenty-ounce big beer. This helps focus your brain on how much you are really drinking and makes over-consumption more difficult. In fact, at a bar where I am a regular, I will often order half beers instead of their standard pint. It sounds strange, but it works.

Strategy Number Four: A Tall Drink of Water!

Like all other parts of your fitness routine, water is an important addition to any happy hour. Water helps hydrate you, it is a filler that helps control cravings, and it is just healthy for you. As mentioned earlier, hydrating yourself with lots of water while you are drinking is a critical part of your happy hour strategy.

When I am at a party or happy hour, I drink one glass of water for every alcoholic drink that I consume. By doing this, the consumption of the high calorie drinks is slowed and it keeps you feeling full which will naturally limit your intake.

Strategy Number Five: Snack Smart!

Usually, drinking alcohol means snacking at the same time. You know how it goes, the tray of drinks arrives, and the group wants to order some appetizers for the table. These snacks often include things that are deep-fried, carb-heavy, covered in melted cheese and dipped in various high-calorie sauces. Everything about that sounds very dangerous to fitness goals. Consuming some kind of food while drinking is a good idea, but it requires smart decisions.

My rule (or guideline really because I tend to fail on this one) is to skip all happy hour foods that are fried, accompanied by chips or otherwise seem excessively unhealthy. Instead, look for vegetables or vegetarian friendly appetizers like fruit, salad or even steamed pot stickers. If you are looking for meat, look for something grilled like chicken satay or other skewers.

Strategy Number Six: There's no Substitution for Substitution!

At nearly every restaurant you may go to, the menu items are mostly just suggestions for how each dish should be enjoyed. There is no rule saying that the way the items are prepared by default is the way that you have to have them. Restaurants are often accommodating of your preferences. You are paying them to do it your way within reason.

When I am at a restaurant, I never hesitate to mix up the preparation for an entree if I don't like how it comes by default. For example, French fries and mashed potatoes are two things that I almost always skip at a restaurant. I substitute fresh vegetables or a salad to remove the unnecessary extras.

This brings me to our old friend, the bread. I am not a zero-carb person. I don't avoid all bread as a rule by any means. That said, I don't always eat bread just because I am ordering a sandwich. If the bread or bun adds to the experience or the flavor, I will absolutely get it and enjoy every bite. If it doesn't add to the experience, I will skip the bread. I simply ask for no bread or for it to be served on a bed of greens. If the server offers to bring bread ahead of the meal, I decline unless somebody I am with wants it.

Not only do you not have to accept the dish as presented, in some cases you don't even have to take the whole dish. Many restaurants will serve you half portions of their entrees where it makes sense. You can also share an entree with the person you are with as another way to throttle the over-eating.

If you aren't sure of your options for how to adjust your food at a restaurant, just ask the question. Severs are very knowledgeable about ways that the dishes on their menus can be altered and are trained how to accommodate a number of special needs. Most chefs and servers are very happy to adjust their dishes in order to make their guests happy.

Please remember one important note. If you are at a restaurant and make several special requests, please make sure to adjust your tip accordingly. They went out of their way to make sure you had the experience you wanted, you should compensate them for that commitment to making you happy. It is only fair.

Strategy Number Seven: Break Time!

I didn't meet my exercise goals every day during my journey. I didn't go to the gym seven days per week. There were days where I only walked two thousand steps. I sat in front of the television. I watched movies or sports and was completely stationary. I don't regret these days even a little bit!

During your journey, it is ok to take some days off of going at it as hard as you can. It is fine to take a day off from your exercise. It is even ok to overeat beyond your calorie target. You just cannot do this often and need to stay focused in general. Plus, it isn't ok to take a day off from being mindful about what you consume.

Not only is it ok to take a day off, but your body will ultimately thank you. Your muscles need time to recover after a hard workout. If you don't take the recovery days, your muscles won't grow as fast, and your weight won't fall as fast. Your body needs the variety in order to most efficiently burn the fat. Plus, your brain needs the flexibility to do different things and let you be in control of your journey versus the other way around.

When you are progressing through a fitness journey, it is important to continue to let yourself live in a way that you enjoy. Don't withhold things from yourself that you really love, just modify your approach to consuming them. This is one of the big differences between fitness projects that succeed and those that fail. Make sure that you succeed by making this something sustainable. You are trying to change your lifestyle, and that is something you have to be able to live with for the long haul.

This week my scale told me that I am 95 pounds lighter than where I started this journey! I am in the home stretch of my 100-pound goal! I am unbelievably excited and proud of myself but I am not going to stop at 100. I will keep going, but I will know that I have won the battle I set out to fight.

OPERATION MELT
WEEK 36

Lesson 9: Nothing Motivates More Than Results

I want to discuss my brain for a minute and how I am wired. If you have ever taken the *Gallup StrengthsFinder* assessment, you know that we are all wired differently and have a unique set of strengths that define how we operate. In Gallup StrengthsFinder the top five strengths are known as your "signature strengths" and are the part of the profile that most thoroughly describes you as a person. I can tell you that I am a big advocate for *Gallup StrenghtsFinder* because I think it is a good way to assess yourself and to leverage your strengths. Plus, I have found my profile to be a pretty accurate description of me.

In my strengths profile, my number one strength, the top of the list of thirty-four is competition. This strength means that I like to keep score. I like measurable performance and to see my score get better, particularly versus others. Said differently, I am numbers-driven when it comes to my performance. When the numbers say that I am winning the competition, I like them even more, and I get energized.

With that spirit of competition in mind, I would like to share the following excerpt from my daily journal from about two weeks after kicking off my *Operation Melt* project:

> *"Yesterday, I had to weigh myself four times because I didn't believe the scale. I have lost twelve pounds in twelve days! Plus, I had to move my belt one more notch tighter because my pants were falling down. I have never used this notch! I have lost a pound a day, and I am seeing visible signs. This is working!"*

I was only a few days into the journey, and I was seeing results. I was winning this competition against myself. I was winning the battle of my life! From that point forward, I was hooked. The very next day, I significantly exceeded all of my daily exercise targets mostly driven by the fact that I was winning.

A couple of months later, I had a follow-up visit with my doctor to check in on a few things. He was very happy with my weight loss rate and how much I had achieved. Then, he said the magic words that fed my competitive mind, "I have had a lot of patients start a weight loss plan, but none of them have ever been as gung ho or as successful as quickly as you."

Boom, I was winning even more!

I rediscovered through the course of my *Operation Melt* journey that success is a huge motivator. When I see results, when I hear that I am killing it, when the numbers are telling me the right story, I want to keep it up. I want to recommit every day. Plus, I want to do even better than I did before.

As I mentioned earlier, I think of my motivation like a success snowball. I work hard and start seeing results. The results make me happy and make me work even harder. This harder work produces bigger results. Then the process repeats itself until I am unstoppable. This is a big part of how I hit my goal in nine months instead of the year that I set out to achieve.

I tell you this story because I think we all have a little bit of the competitive spirit inside of us. I think we are all motivated when we start seeing those results. Nothing is as much of a motivator as success.

But, success in your fitness journey is gradual. It will take some time before you start really seeing physical changes. That is why I chose the "measure everything" approach to my *Operation Melt* project. I knew that the numbers would be the first place I saw results. I was right, and it made all the difference. It only took me a few days to start seeing results on the scale and in the KPIs (Key Performance Indicators) that I was tracking. From that point forward, I was hooked!

So, be very diligent about tracking your KPIs, and the numbers won't lie. You will start seeing success in the KPIs first, and you can celebrate that success. Then, use today's success to build the momentum to keep up the hard work tomorrow.

Athlete?!
My doctor referred to me as an
"athlete" this week. This really
surprised me, because I have
never thought of myself as an
athlete. Could it be that I
became an athlete and didn't
know it?

OPERATION MELT
WEEK 37

Lesson 10: I Am Amazing And You Are Too!

When I first started this book, I introduced myself with the following words, "My name is Tony, and I am just a guy living a normal, middle class, urban life in Columbus, Ohio."

When I started my *Operation Melt* project, this is really how I thought about myself. I was just a guy and nothing special. This is how I approached my life, my job, my health and fitness, and pretty much everything else. I was doing my best to succeed in the various aspects of my life. I had done some impressive things in the past, but I, myself, wasn't anything impressive. I was wrong. I am more than average. I am amazing!

I have learned that I really can accomplish anything that I set out to do, as long as it is important to me. I never thought I could lose over one-hundred pounds. I never thought that I could begin to address the weight issue that has plagued me for as long as I can remember. But I set a goal, built a plan and did it! I can do it again and again, and I am unstoppable once I decide to be that way. I didn't think I had it in me, but here we are.

I actually had no real appreciation of how big of a deal a hundred-pound weight loss in nine months really was. Especially when it felt natural and right to me at the time. As I talked to people who had tried it and as I continued to research, I became truly aware of how rare it is to achieve this. Oh, there are people out there who have done it even faster, and I am in awe of them. But I am not envious by any means, because I did mine the way I wanted to do it. This included a fair amount of bourbon and beer along the way. Imagine how fast I would have dropped the pounds without continuing to drink and eat crappy foods. But for me, I probably wouldn't have stuck with it if that were the case.

For the first time in a long time, I know that my experiences are valuable, and I have something to contribute. I want to tell my story to others. I want to inspire others to start their own journeys, and I want to help them win. I want to help eliminate the obesity epidemic in America one person at a time. I know that I have already eliminated one since I am under the threshold of "obese" for the first time in as long as I can remember.

Along the way in my journey, I found that I was changing my brain, not just my body, when I lost my job. When I suddenly was downsized from a company where I had worked and contributed for ten years, I had choices of how to react. I could easily have been devastated and let that roadblock become my focus. I could have stopped caring about fitness and could have let myself spend every day on the couch watching television. I could have let the loss of a job negatively impact my view of my self-worth. If it had happened a year or two before *Operation Melt*, that would have been a distinct possibility. But not when I had invested in my fitness journey.

Through *Operation Melt,* I learned that I was bigger than my job. I had lots of non-career goals in life, which was something I couldn't say before I started this journey. I came to know that I was valuable, my time was valuable, my ideas were valuable, that people would benefit from me sharing my perspective. So, I became determined to do that whenever I could.

As you may have deduced, I increased confidence during my journey. I also improved how much I value myself. After all, you can't do the work necessary to lose one-hundred plus pounds unless you value yourself enough to start and stick with the plan. But, this chapter is not about my bragging and boasting, though that can be fun sometimes.

I want you to understand that you are an amazing person as am I! We are all capable of so much more than we are doing today. We have more strength in us than we can possibly know. If we find things that are important to us, and we decide to change them, then we will change them. Think about the countless stories you hear each day about people who have accomplished something astounding. Whether you look at great inventors, athletes or anybody else who has accomplished something big, they started at one idea, one inspiring goal. They had such a goal and something that was important to them. They committed and went for it.

If you want to lose one-hundred pounds, you can. Simply commit to it, have a strong enough business case for why it is important, and measure your progress every day. Just believe in yourself and get started. Then, stick with it when you encounter the issues and get past them. You will be successful.

So, let me finish this chapter by rewriting the opening paragraph from the beginning of this book the way I should have written it.

My name is Tony, and I am a pretty amazing guy who can accomplish anything. I have many meaningful accomplishments in my life and want to tell you a story about a recent one: I lost over one-hundred pounds in nine months. The best part is that I did this my way and was still able to maintain my lifestyle filled with fun and enjoyment. I couldn't have done it without the support, partnership and love from my amazing wife of eighteen years, Liz. We started out as best friends for about four years, then decided to get married and have lived happily ever after in Columbus, Ohio. While we have many of the same normal stresses that everybody else has, including demanding jobs, we really enjoy our life. My hope with this book is to help you realize that you too are amazing and can accomplish your fitness goals through a fairly simple process based on project management best practices. Let's get started!

The big day finally arrived! I stepped on the scale this morning, and I have lost 100.2 pounds in less than 9 months! I didn't really know how I would feel the day I hit my goal. I can tell you that my first feeling was utter surprise. Then I rewarded myself with a killer workout.

OPERATION MELT
WEEK 38

Part 4: Operation Melt Phase 2

Well... Now What?

I unexpectedly hit my hundred-pound weight loss goal just before the nine-month anniversary of starting my journey. This was an exciting moment for me, and I bragged about it and celebrated it a bit. But after I did that, I headed to the gym for a workout. In fact, the workout the morning that I hit that milestone was a pretty fierce one by my standards to that point. I clearly decided that I wasn't done yet, but I needed to figure out what came next in my journey.

Once I had completed the first phase of my *Operation Melt* project, as measured by achieving my goal, I decided it was time for Phase Two. The second phase would include several new goals and scope items. The first focus was to continue to more weight loss. I decided to keep going for the full year that I set as my initial timeline. I wanted to keep losing weight with a revised goal to be under a total weight of two-hundred pounds by the one-year point. The next goal was to get under two-hundred pounds and then to switch to a maintenance mode.

Phase Two of *Operation Melt* would not just be about losing weight. I had bigger goals than just losing another twenty-five pounds. To me, and my newly found confidence, that felt like too small of a goal after losing one-hundred pounds. Phase Two included the following goals:

- Building muscle and shaping my new smaller body to be visibly muscular

- Working with a personal trainer to ensure that I correctly and safely focused on working my entire body

- Participating in my first organized and professionally timed race

- Doing at least one pull-up and at least twenty quality push-ups.

- Writing a book to help other people follow in my footsteps and be successful with their own journeys. If you are reading this, I have been successful with this item!

- Going to my next annual check-up with my doctor and have him say, "Wow!" when we compare all of the data year-over-year.

My hope is that *Operation Melt* is never done and that I just continue to improve my health and fitness. If I keep it up, I will break free from the trend of early deaths in my family.

My final goal for Phase Two of my *Operation Melt* journey was to multiply the success by helping others. I want everybody to be able to set reasonable and aggressive fitness goals and achieve them. I want everybody to feel the sense of accomplishment that I felt that morning when

I stepped on the scale and it told me I was a Rock Star. I want everybody to learn how their digital devices can help solve America's obesity epidemic, rather than to contribute to it.

I want you to be healthier and more fit than you ever imagined possible!

Last week's 100-pounds victory marked the end of the first phase of my Operation Melt journey, and I killed that first goal. Now, I am moving into phase 2. Most importantly I am not stopping, I am committed and will continue what I started. I am going to try for 125 pounds in 1 year!

OPERATION MELT
WEEK 39

Post-Audit: 9 Months Later

A project is about more than the process and steps used for implementation; projects are about results. That is why many project management offices have instituted a post-implementation audit (or, simply, "post-audit") policy. A post-audit is a review of the results of a project at some point after it has been implemented. The goal of this review is to determine whether the project has delivered, or is on track to deliver, its intended results.

For my Operation Melt project I completed my post-audit nine months after my initial results had been achieved.

5, 4, 3, 2, 1 ... happy new year!

Right after midnight, just eighteen months after beginning my Operation Melt journey, I officially brought my weight loss journey to an end. We counted down, I kissed Liz, we toasted with some sparkling wine, and then I switched my tracking apps to maintenance mode instead of weight loss. It was a big and proud moment that I never thought I would experience in my life.

The Weight is Gone for Good

Let me start by telling you that I have kept the weight off. Even bigger than keeping the weight off, I continued to lose weight right up to the point when I switched to maintenance mode. I lost a total of around 130 pounds, forty-percent, of my total body weight.

I only stopped losing weight because I listened to my body, and it told me that I had lost all the weight I could safely lose. My rate of loss had slowed to almost zero, and many other indicators told me that I lost all that I could.

Unfortunately, I was not happy with the actual numbers at this stopping point because my BMI is still in the "overweight" category. I know that BMI is a general guideline, and I am not overweight any longer. It is honestly very strange to say that!

But the weight wasn't the only change!

My Body has Changed

Not only did I lose weight, but an increased focus on weight-training and work with a personal trainer brought increased definition to my muscles. The muscle growth was so significant that I was able to deadlift my body weight just a few months after not being able to lift a hundred pounds.

These changes in my body are part of why I stopped my focus on weight loss. After all of the focus on shaping and toning my muscles, I achieved a body-fat percentage of just twelve percent. This body-fat percentage places me firmly in the "athletes" category. More on that to follow later.

I Ran That First 5k, With a Twist

I mentioned a few times throughout this book that I wanted to get to the point where I could comfortably run a 5k race. It felt like a good goal given where I was in my running abilities when I hit the one-hundred pounds lost mark. But achieving the ability to run a 5k required serious training given that I could barely run a mile without resting.

I finally achieved the goal of running my first 5k race just three months after reaching my one-hundred pound milestone. But, like every other aspect of this journey, I decided I wanted to do my first 5k on my own terms. Simply signing up for a 5k race just didn't feel special enough given what I had just accomplished, so I did my first 5k a little differently than most.

On the one-year anniversary of starting my journey I hosted the Operation Melt First Time 5k race. I ran my first 5k with about a dozen of my friends on a warm June morning. The race was a fundraiser for a local nonprofit and was a fantastic time. My time was really great, I was very happy with my performance, and I was super excited to achieve this goal with my friends — one of my friends even made us all "finishers" medals.

I Really Became an Athlete

I completed my first 5k, but I didn't stop there. I began running, on average, one organized race per month. I completed multiple 5k races, a 4-miler race and a 10k race, and my times just kept getting better. I was officially a runner, but I had one more big milestone to check off the list.

In October, just sixteen months after starting my journey, I participated in the Columbus Marathon by running my first half-marathon. This was not an easy race at all, and I very nearly quit twice due to issues with cramping. But I didn't quit. I kept pushing through the pain and the struggles, and I crossed the finish line in two hours and forty-four minutes.

Finishing a half marathon was a big and emotional accomplishment for me. It was validation that I didn't just get lucky and happen into weight loss. I am not just an occasional runner without skill and talent. I am an athlete and will only get better from here!

I Really Became a Writer

I am sure it is quite clear that I have become a writer given that you are reading the final chapter of my book. But my writing isn't limited just to a single book.

Every day I produce fitness, project management, leadership and other content in my Operation Melt blog and social media.

You may wonder why I spend so much time producing content, particularly content that can get pretty personal. I do it because I am hopeful that something I have created will connect with a reader and help her or him get a step closer to achieving life-changing goals. I have received several pieces of feedback that this is exactly what has happened many times. It feels great every time this happens.

I Discovered Who I Am

I have talked a lot through this book about my weight loss, but this journey turned out not to just be about what I lost, it is also about what I gained.

I gained more knowledge about who I am and what is important to me. I love using my knowledge, skills and talents to help people achieve their goals. I have a passion for turning wishes into goals, goals into plans, and plans into reality — either my own or other people's goals.

I gained more self-confidence than I have had in years. I am not only passionate about helping to make goals come true for others, I also know that I can do it. No matter the goal, my project management based approach can help make it come to life.

I am completely unstoppable, and you can be too!

Are you ready to change your life?

Oh my god! I just finished a half marathon! It hit me like a ton of bricks that I just finished a half marathon 16 months after being 325 pounds. This was a big f-ing victory! This was a clear win in my journey. I couldn't believe how far I had come. That's when the tears started flowing.

OPERATION MELT
WEEK 70